vastu

TRANSCENDENTAL HOME DESIGN
IN HARMONY WITH NATURE

vastu

TRANSCENDENTAL HOME DESIGN
IN HARMONY WITH NATURE

SHERRI SILVERMAN

Gibbs Smith, Publisher
TO ENRICH AND INSPIRE HUMANKIND
Salt Lake City | Charleston | Santa Fe | Santa Barbara

First Edition
11 10 09 08 07   5 4 3 2 1

Text © 2007 Sherri Silverman
Photographs © as noted on page 157
Paintings © Sherri Silverman, unless otherwise noted
Illustrations on pages 32 and 41 © Erin Englund

Published by
Gibbs Smith, Publisher
P.O. Box 667
Layton, Utah 84041

Orders: 1.800.835.4993
www.gibbs-smith.com

Designed by Black Eye Design • www.blackeye.com
Printed and bound in China

Library of Congress Cataloging-in-Publication Data

Silverman, Sherri.
  Vastu : transcendental home design in harmony with nature / Sherri Silverman.— 1st ed.
      p. cm.
  Includes bibliographical references and index.
  ISBN-13: 978-1-4236-0132-6
  ISBN-10: 1-4236-0132-7
  1. Architecture, Domestic—Psychological aspects. 2. Interior
architecture—Psychological aspects. 3. Interior decoration—Indic
influences. 4. Vastu. I. Title.

NA7125.S56 2007
133.3'33--dc22
                        2007011270

लोकानां हितकाम्यया

lokānām hitakāmyayā

for the comfort and fulfillment of the aspirations of humanity

Contents

Acknowledgments

I thank my clients and everyone I have learned from for their contributions and encouragement. I would not be able to present Vastu authentically without my background in meditation and Vedic studies with Maharishi Mahesh Yogi. I thank my spiritual teacher, Sri Sri Ravi Shankar, for attention and grace showered upon me. The practices of Sahaj Samadhi Meditation and Sudarshan Kriya I learned and taught through his Art of Living Foundation enabled me to properly approach this work. I also acknowledge the late Ajit Mookerjee, whom I knew from his wonderful books on yoga art and tantra art and then studied with when he visited my home in Santa Fe. My approach to Purusha-Prakriti is based on his writing.

Gratitude goes to Mary Chambers, my Web site designer, who encouraged me to write this book, saying it was where my "greatest convergence is . . . the combination of creativity, deep understanding of inner workings of abstract forces, and teaching."

I thank my mom, Faye Price, for her support, even though she didn't quite understand what I was up to. Her father wrote books, and she and my own father expected that I would too.

My friend Bija Bennett, author of *Emotional Yoga*, supported the writing of this book by giving me her old Mac, which I named Durga. On short notice, Bija allowed photographs to be taken of her beautiful home and office, which we had worked on with Vastu principles.

Vijaya Tensei helped with technical support and thoughtful tutoring when I first got the Mac. I thank Vijaya for his generosity, his devotion to Durga, and the attention he lavished on my iBook, Tara, which came as an unexpected gift from my stepdad, Sam Price. Vijaya also aided me when Tara morphed into Dhana Lakshmi, my current MacBook.

Dr. V. Ganapati Sthapati, the world's greatest authority on Vastu, graciously responded to e-mailed questions in the years I studied his books before being able to study with him and ask questions directly. I found the dedication of this book on page 301 of his *Building Architecture of Sthapatya Veda*.

Vastu Architect Michael Borden offered a clear online Vastu theory course and spent time answering endless questions in a straightforward, pragmatic way.

I thank Ayurvedic Vaidya Rama Kant Mishra for encouraging my study with him, for knowledge gained in his Ayurvedic Transdermal Marma Therapy workshop, and for his permission to use material in this book, including the components of prana.

Many friends lent me spaces in which to write this book. Client Teresa Archuleta-Spires loaned me her peaceful Española studio. Paula Baker-Laporte and Robert Laporte offered their Tesuque Econest guesthouse when I needed another retreat in which to birth this book; they also provided an enthusiastic reading of the manuscript. Susan Crutchfield's Santa Fe guesthouse was an additional writing retreat; I thank Susan for magically being there at the right time, divinely guided.

I appreciate insight gained from conversations with Marcus Schmieke and his permission to reproduce some of the yantras he has researched and produced. My friend Laura Trisiano suggested valuable additions to this book and supported me with her constant belief in my creativity. Cheryl Silver provided evening walks and other sustenance. Jessie Mercay was one of the first to encourage me to write this book; she has since become a Vastu builder and founded a Vastu school. Blaine Watson passed along anecdotes about Vastu homes. Miriam Austin, author of *Yoga for Wimps* and *Cool Yoga Tricks*, provided encouragement, insightful suggestions, and support for the publishing process.

Vedic scholar David Frawley (Vamadeva Shastri) gave support on many levels. I am grateful to Vamadeva for books, discussions about Vedic knowledge, Sanskrit translations, rejuvenating hikes, and connecting me with colleagues, clients, and publications.

Photographer Kimberly Wright blessed me by, among other things, taking photographs of spaces I had worked on for an article in *Santa Fe Trend* Magazine. Kimberly also contributed my portrait photograph.

I am so delighted to have found and worked with my main photographer, Erika Blumenfeld. Her technical skill and artistic talent and her ability to convey beauty and spirituality in a photo helped create this book the way I intended it to be. Our happy collaboration on photo shoots was fun and productive beyond what either of us could have accomplished on our own.

I am also truly grateful to all the wonderful people who allowed us to photograph in their homes; I thank all of them, especially Jane Brodie, who took extra time to help us create and capture truly lovely images. The photoshoots were enhanced by rugs, tables, lamps, and accessories graciously loaned by Asian Adobe, G. Coles-Christensen Rug Merchants, Oriental Rug Resource, Pacific Artefacts, and Sequoia.

Sandra Crowley, author of *Wabi Sabi Style*; Paula Baker-Laporte and Robert Laporte, authors of *Econest*; and Sunamita Lim, author of *Chinese Style*, gave me advice on publishing and connected me with publisher Gibbs Smith. I thank Gibbs for his vision and belief in the value of Vastu as a world wisdom tradition. GSP CEO Christopher Robbins, Editorial Vice President Suzanne Taylor, and my attentive editor, Lisa Anderson—who guided me through the publication process to create a better book—must all be acknowledged for bringing this knowledge in a beautiful way to a wider audience. I have been graced with wonderful support from friends, teachers, clients, and associates, and I am very grateful.

Sherri Silverman

Introduction

Vastu is India's ancient Vedic tradition of design, architecture, and sacred space. Today everyone is familiar with how yoga presents a path to greater harmony, health, energy, and joy in life. As the "yoga of design," Vastu offers another way to achieve these benefits by working in alignment with nature when creating and enhancing the spaces in which we live. Since yoga, meditation, Ayurveda, and Jyotish (Vedic astrology) are now popular, it is only natural that this valuable system of architecture and design is recognized and explored for the enrichment it can give human life. My Vastu design clients report greater ease, prosperity, happiness, and a delight in being in their homes unlike what they had experienced beforehand.

I was led to Vastu through my interest in Vedic knowledge, sacred space, meditation, and my lifelong sensitivity to beauty and the effect of my environment upon my state of being. I am a visual artist, so embellishing spaces and making them my own started at an early age. When I was four, I insisted that prospective buyers of my family's Atlanta house see the paintings I had done in my bedroom closet. In 1975–76, I began learning about Vastu. This grew into an increasing fascination with creating sacred space. At that time I was in a Vedic Studies doctoral program in Switzerland at MERU, Maharishi European Research University, studying yoga, meditation, *pranayama* (breathing techniques), research into consciousness, Patanjali's *Yoga Sutras*, and related material with Maharishi Mahesh Yogi. While I was on this course, I met a woman called Mother Olsen, who had hosted Maharishi when he first came to the United States. One day she mentioned to me, "Angels don't like dirt!" This may not sound like a big revelation, but it made a big impression on me, since I noticed that cleaning revs up the energy in a room. Maharishi suggested that we keep our rooms clean and orderly, since it welcomed the divine into the space. He said that your desk should not be placed up against a wall since that would restrict creativity. Another point he brought up was that the best placement for the head of a bed is in the east, and that having your head in the north would be draining and age one more quickly, due to the effect of the earth's electromagnetic grid. These suggestions turned out to be elements of Vastu. Maharishi also told my Vedic Studies doctoral group that we would intuitively perceive the errors in the translation of Vedic knowledge, perhaps because of the development of consciousness and intuition from the meditation and other spiritual practices we were doing. I have learned to trust this.

I received my Ph.D. in Creativity, the Arts, and the Sacred/Application of Asian Concepts from the Union Institute & University in 1996. My study of sacred architecture, creative energy pouring into the world through a central point, concentric squares, the effect of beauty, Asian art, and other elements of Vastu inform this book. My doctoral research was based on what I had learned from three teachers: Maharishi Mahesh Yogi, who introduced me to the bountiful benefits of meditation and Vedic knowledge; Sri Sri Ravi Shankar, my spiritual teacher since 1990; and Ajit Mookerjee, an

expert on the art of India and Tantra. My sensitivity to beauty and environments and other components of my true work came together.

Other friends Mangla Sharda and Priya Mookerjee (one of Ajit's daughters) generously helped me with my doctoral studies. They had built a beautiful home in Santa Fe using some Vastu principles that Mangla, who was an architect, had incorporated into their plans. At this point, another friend made suggestions for my home on a copy of the floor plan. I got excited, since every time I implemented these points, I could notice a definite energy shift and greater sparkle in the air. I began reading material on Feng Shui and remembered the many references to Vastu in my doctoral research. At the same time I began learning additional points of Vastu from my spiritual teacher Sri Sri Ravi Shankar.

I started making recommendations to friends about their homes, and they had dramatic, overnight improvements. Victoria slept better. Men started showing up at Martha's door the very next day. Clearly the universe was sending me signs and encouragement to trust focusing in this direction. I realized that my friends were right—I was really good at this. It was innate. I began doing home, business, and garden Vastu design consultations and continued my study of this great world wisdom tradition. I had been using "Transcendence" for my visual art career; once I launched my Web site, the two aspects of Vastu design and visual art—both of which produce a healing, sacred effect—came together as "Transcendence Design."

One of my primary sources in Vastu matters is Dr. V. Ganapati Sthapati, the world's foremost reviver of this knowledge. The best books to read on the subject of authentic Vastu building are by Sthapati. Since this current book is mainly about how to improve your existing space, not all of it is based on Sthapati; some of the techniques I share come from related fields. My research on yantras, the sacred geometry of the Vedic tradition, includes the work of friends and colleagues Ajit Mookerjee, Madhu Khanna, and Marcus Schmieke. I continue to study Vastu and dialogue with colleagues and Vedic scholars. From this will emerge even more useful knowledge that we can apply to the architectural spaces that shelter and nourish us.

This book includes Sanskrit to add flavor and the support of sacred sound. I use the most widely used transliteration scheme for this ancient and sacred alphabet, IAST (International Alphabet of Sanskrit Transliteration), in order to provide an easy phonetic understanding of the pronunciation. Here are a few simple tips: If there is a long mark over a vowel, pronounce it a bit longer than the same vowel without the long mark. "Th" is not pronounced like we do in English in the words "thus" and "there"; instead, pronounce it more like our letter "t." An "s" with a dot underneath or an accent mark above it is pronounced "sh" as in "shelter."

I hope to give the reader a practical introduction to Vastu, along with understanding of the basic symbolic, archetypal concepts. I have done my best to discern what is accurate. My intention is to explain Vastu concepts free of superstition, rigidity, and distortions. Some of this material is contemporary extrapolation based on current needs and the fact that Vastu requires attunement with nature. Plastic and synthetic materials were not an issue when Mayan, the legendary founder of Vastu, was alive. During those early years of Vastu, the selection of land and construction always followed Vastu guidelines. The primary texts do not give much advice on rectification. In general, these rectification suggestions are based on fundamental Vastu principles and definitely work, but exact prediction of effects is not as scientifically grounded as those of Vastu-constructed buildings.

There are five sections to this guide to Vastu, which explain how to improve the beauty, functionality, and comfort of your home. Section One explains what Vastu is and how it truly creates what we need: home sanctuaries that increase our sense of inner peace and well-being. Since many people are familiar with Feng Shui, there is an explanation of how they relate and differ. Section Two goes into detail about the components and factors to consider when creating a Vastu home, so that you can gain greater support for your relationships, health, finance, and career. Section Three walks you through the house and yard and gives tips for the arrangement and décor of all of these areas. Section Four introduces related, complementary techniques that can be applied to bless and energize the house. Section Five offers resources for further study, a detailed glossary, bibliography, and index.

I hope the offering of this book is a worthwhile, true, and practical contribution to this field of knowledge that so intimately impacts our lives.

Sherri Silverman

Rudrabhishekha in Devi, pastel painting on paper, Sherri Silverman.

Section I

what is vastu?

Sacred space reminds us of our true nature and brings us back to center, giving us the support we need to go back out into the stress and uncertainty of the world. Our environments are extensions of our inner self: they have the potential to nourish our soul's expression instead of creating obstacles to the fulfillment of our desires. We can enhance our connection with inner peace and joy through attention to the structure of our home and work environments.

Vastu is the system of architecture, design, and sacred space from ancient India's Vedic tradition. It is both architecture and the art of how to honor and fill the space enclosed within that form. Vastu design requires beauty, comfort, and practicality; the use of natural materials; and attunement with nature through the honoring of the five elements and the nine directions. Vastu contains guidelines for an extraordinarily wide range of arts and practical design, including dance and the creation of vehicles and gardens.

Most books will say that the main Vastu texts are *Mayamatam* and *Manasara*. My own response to reading these medieval textbooks is that they seem to contain erroneous material. Indian architect Ganapati Sthapati, the foremost contemporary authority on Vastu, says that *Manasara* is only sixty percent accurate. This book contains only what I feel is authentic and effective.

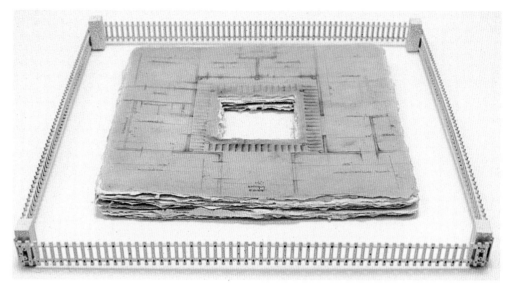

Sthapatya Ved, artist Madeline de Joly's depiction of the structural principles of Vedic architecture. A virtual tour of her exhibition *Veda and the Vedic Literature* at the Graduate Theological Union in Berkeley is at www.madelinedejoly.com.

The Sanskrit word "Vastu" means "energy" or "imperishable substance." "Vaastu" refers to the humanly built forms that are filled with that space energy, what Ganapati Sthapati calls "embodied energy." The form and the space within the form are intimately connected and affect each other. Vastu creates true sacred space that is both spiritually and scientifically based.

There is an expression in Sanskrit, "Vastu reva vaastu," which means that unbounded pure consciousness, the unmanifest source of all manifestation, transforms into the manifest material world. In other words, as Einstein discovered, energy becomes matter. It is these same laws of nature, or subtle mechanics of creation, that are utilized in Vastu guidelines. Thus, Vastu is based on physics and is a mathematical technology.

Vastu comes from the same tradition as yoga, meditation, Ayurveda, and Jyotish (Vedic astrology). Like meditation and yoga, Vastu is universal and useful for people everywhere. As the yoga of design, Vastu brings greater balance, health, harmony, inner peace, a sense of well-being, and unity to our bodies, minds, emotions, and lives.

Meditation connects us with the source of pure consciousness; Vastu enhances this effect and connects us with the source through proper design.

Ayurveda, the science of life, gives us knowledge for health. As the science of design and architecture, Vastu gives us knowledge for the health of buildings, which profoundly affects our health, happiness, and prosperity—and the health of the environment.

Jyotish gives knowledge of the influences of the cosmos on our lives, emotions, relationships, prosperity, career, and health. Vastu can help protect us from negative influences in all of these areas.

A house that stands in my heart

My cathedral of silence

Ma cathédrale de silence

Une maison dressée au coeur[1]

—Poet Jean Laroche

India's Vedic tradition has been credited with birthing this great tool for our growth, prosperity, and tranquility in life, but its roots are more ancient than what is called the Vedic period in Indian history. Since Vastu is over ten thousand years old, it predates Hinduism and organized religion. Knowledge of Vastu is part of our planetary heritage. It has the potential to revolutionize lives by creating buildings that, as living organisms, fully support our health, growth, and happiness instead of being the cause of many of our problems, as we see with today's "sick" buildings.

Vastu: Creating Home as Sanctuary

Vastu helps create the peace and stability we need to have success in life on all levels, spiritual and material. Having homes that completely support, protect, and nourish us has not been experienced on a broad scale. Vastu offers us homes, public buildings, and work spaces that actually do this.

Vastu's purpose is to align our architectural spaces with the beneficial effects of the laws of nature and the influence of earth and cosmic energies. Vastu views a building as a living entity that protects and nourishes our lives rather than merely "a machine for living," as twentieth-century architect Le Corbusier once characterized the house. Vastu works in an honoring partnership with nature rather than with an arrogant attitude of controlling or conquering nature, which has devastated our larger home, the environment of this planet.

Vastu is a science and an art. As a numerical technology, it is math- and physics-based, which enables the Vastu expert to utilize the subtle mechanics of creation for a harmoniously aligned building. How this is done is discussed at the end of Section Two in "*Ayadi*: Calculations to Fit the Individual." Vastu creates buildings that powerfully generate energy for the benefit of the building's inhabitants. Authentic Vastu building immerses us in living in harmony with nature and ourselves. Through its adherence to natural laws, a "living organism" is constructed instead of a dead building.

Vastu's use for rectification of existing buildings is potent, even though it was not designed for this purpose. When you change an architectural structure that was not designed according to Vastu, the already present dissonant energies prevent the prediction of the rectification's exact results. My experience and the experience of my clients and colleagues, however, is that applying Vastu to existing structures produces tremendous improvements in architectural spaces and in the quality of life of those who live and work in them. This is greatly needed. Our contemporary world is exhausting. We are bombarded with challenges to the health of our minds, bodies, and emotions. Chemical, noise, and electromagnetic pollution have a significant deleterious effect upon us. We long for the healing effects of beauty and peace. Uncertainty in our world has created an intent interest in sacred space, sacred architecture, and sacred life. Our lives and the buildings we live in should exemplify this ideal. Sacred architecture, most profoundly and purely exemplified by the Vastu tradition, provides

[Our house] had a heart,
and a soul, and eyes to see us
with; and approvals, and
solicitudes, and deep sympathies;
it was of us, and we were in
its confidence, and lived in
its grace and in the peace of
its benediction . . .
We could not enter it unmoved.

—MARK TWAIN

sanctuary for the shattered soul, especially today, when we hunger for an innermost chamber both within ourselves and within the honored temple of wherever we live. This is what in Sanskrit is called *garbha-griha*, "womb chamber" or "innermost chamber," a loving and supportive environment that provides both protection and nourishment. Authentic Vastu creates this.

In dreams, homes are often symbolic of our physical bodies. We spend a lot of time being encased or literally housed in them. Vastu reflects this symbolism by referring to the structure of our homes as representative of our own bodies; what goes on in the one affects the other. All the sciences of yoga, meditation, Ayurveda, and Vastu view the body as a universe in miniature. Mayan, the legendary originator of Vastu knowledge, is attributed with coining the aphorisms "As in macro, so in micro," and "As above, so below." Our own little universes of body and home reflect and are composed of the same forces that compose the vast cosmic universe.

Vastu creates homes in which *prana* (subtle, sparkly, universal life energy: what Chinese systems of Feng Shui and oriental medicine call *ch'i*) flows freely and there are no structural elements that predispose us to illness or problems in life. Existing health problems ease up and can even clear up from being in buildings constructed according to true Vastu. Vastu can be applied to rectify energetic imbalances in existing homes, although building a new house according to Vastu principles produces a much more powerfully nourishing environment.

There is great benefit from having your built space aligned with cosmic forces. In the words of the Vastu text *Shilpa Vidya Rahasyopanisad*, "The worlds acquire prosperity and all-auspiciousness by means of Shilpa." *Shilpa* refers to this sacred system of creating in harmony with nature through Vastu. Here is a great story sent to me in a letter written about California Vastu homes that were spared by the 2003 fires:

Friends who are visiting from their Vastu home in Ramona, California, the epicenter of the San Diego fires, had some heroic stories about the Cedar Fire. That fire is now three hundred thousand acres and destroyed eight hundred homes. It started a few miles east of Ramona and roared up the steep hillside, overwhelming the community. More than one hundred homes were destroyed. The astonishing news is that none of the six Vastu houses were touched. My friends' house is perched on a hilltop. The house just to the north was destroyed as well as a seven-thousand-square-foot stone house just to the west. Their shrubs outside the Vastu fence were burned, but not the fence or house. The fire passed right around the home inexplicably. Another couple has a Vastu house under construction which abuts the national forest. The fire came up to their lot, destroyed their trailer outside the Vastu fence, but didn't singe the temporary rope Vastu fence as it went around the property.

The home next door, the first Vastu house built in Ramona, was sold to people who did not know about Vastu's protective benefits. The new owner built a non-Vastu-compliant fence to surround a pool on the wrong side. That fence was burned, the pool damaged, and the

In July 2006 I participated in a ceremony to lay the cornerstone for a small Vastu building in Las Vegas, New Mexico. The group of us had gotten very little sleep, had risen at four a.m., and then got lost driving to this location with inadequate directions on an unseasonably cool day. Needless to say, we were a little out of kilter. However, the laying of the cornerstones created the beginning of a true Vastu structure, which as a living organism emanated an amazing feeling into the environment. Even this small Vastu beginning of a building created an incredibly blissful, carefree feeling of ease and camaraderie among the group. I found it impressive to experience this from a building that had barely begun. Clearly, Vastu has great potency for harmonizing the environment.

 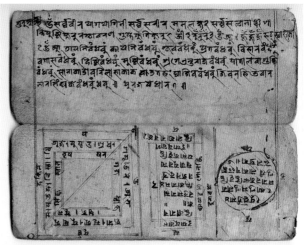

Handwritten and illustrated Vastu
manuscripts, Nepal, c. 1800.

house itself in jeopardy when the burning pool fence threatened to set the house on fire. Just in time, the fire department arrived to put out the small fire before it could do more damage. Another family's Vastu property located a few miles away also survived.

Building according to Vastu guidelines also creates a more comfortable home, as I found out first-hand when visiting friends. We walked to the neighbors' house to water their plants, since they were out of town. Whereas my friends' home was naturally cool, even at the height of the summer's heat, I started sweating literally the minute we walked inside the house next door, which was designed conventionally with no attention to Vastu principles of placement, materials, and design. It was a clear demonstration of the effectiveness of Vastu principles and made me even more convinced of the necessity of this knowledge.

Vastu's History and Influence

Vastu originated with Mayan, who is also referred to as Brahmarishi Maya Danava, Mayasura, and Mamuni Mayan. Mayan was a brilliant and creative historical figure with a possible legendary overlay. His identity is blurred with that of the architect of the gods, Vishwakarman, whose work is described in the epics of India, the *Mahabharata* and the *Ramayana*. Mayan lived in a land to the south of India over twelve thousand years ago, around 10,000 BCE, before the continental drift. His knowledge of sacred architecture spread throughout India and other parts of the planet through his travels and those of his students. Ganapati Sthapati visited Central America a few years ago and found convincing evidence that Mayan journeyed across the ocean and brought Vastu (and his name) with him.

Bodhisattva fresco painting by artist
Karla Refojo.

Mayan pyramids in Mexico follow Vastu techniques, guidelines, and measurements in detail, as does stonework in Peru. This sounds like the stuff of myths, and it may be. However, it is useful to keep an open mind: Some legends have turned out to be true, as in the example of the mythical ancient Chinese Qin dynasty and its emperor Shihuangdi, which remained legendary until farmers digging a well in a field in 1974 found the mound that contained Shihuangdi's mausoleum complex.

Compliance with Vastu guidelines can be seen in present-day Pakistan in the ruins of Mohenjo-Daro and other towns of the Indus Valley-Harappan civilization of around 2700 to 1500 BCE, which featured homes with central courtyards, indoor plumbing, and streets laid out in a grid pattern. It is found as well as in the design of the Taj Mahal, the quintessential architectural symbol of India that, while built by Islamic rulers, shows evidence of acknowledging Vastu guidelines.

Vastu and other knowledge from India were known in Greece and Rome. Merchants journeyed on trade routes to bring medicines, spices, and other treasures from India to Europe, and some of the great knowledge of India's Vedic tradition came back to Europe with them. The Roman writer Pliny clearly valued India's knowledge; he prescribed *tulsi*, or holy basil, and wrote about the amount of money that went from Rome to India to pay for medicinal herbs.

Prasanna Kumar Acharya, a twentieth-century translator of *Manasara*, theorized that the architect Vitruvius copied the chapter names and their sequence from *Manasara*. The Italian Renaissance architect Andrea Palladio created buildings with a harmonious radial symmetry in the 1560s that appear to be based on Vastu as well. His Villa Rotunda in Vicenza, Italy, features a central circular space inside two concentric squares, with entry extensions in all four directions.

George Washington followed architectural models from Palladio and others who were influenced by Vastu. He "believed that architectural proportions were set by divine law . . . The careful measurement of his new rooms [was] . . . about symbolically constructing God's will."[2] Proportions "set by divine law"—natural law—and modulated on the grid pattern of the Vastu Purusha Mandala create buildings that are alive, supportive, and nourishing.

Vastu and Feng Shui

Feng Shui (pronounced "fung shway") is the architectural and interior design system from China that is literally translated as "wind and water." Like Vastu, Feng Shui's intention is to enable optimal beneficial results in life and the healthy, unobstructed flow of *ch'i*, or "universal life energy" (called *prana* in Sanskrit), within a built space.

Since ancient China had a strong tradition of ancestor worship, Feng Shui was originally intended for ideal placement of grave sites so that people could gain the most benefit from their ancestors. This later developed into a system of placement for homes and other buildings. Vastu, on the other

This Japanese-style bedroom is a lovely option for a Vastu home, since all styles of interior design can be compatible with Vastu.

hand, began as a scientific and spiritually based system of design for all kinds of buildings: temples, businesses, homes.

Vastu began thousands of years before Feng Shui and is part of Feng Shui's origin. Vastu is not Indian Feng Shui, although it has sometimes been explained that way. Knowledge of Vastu traveled along the Silk Road and on sea routes with merchants and monks. Vastu influenced native East and Southeast Asian traditions, as did other fields of knowledge from India: Hinduism, Buddhism, Jyotish (astrology), and Ayurveda. There are even legends that Buddha himself traveled to East and Southeast Asia and could have brought India's great knowledge systems with him. Emperor Ashoka, a famous convert to Buddhism, sent specialists in India's traditions to Southeast and East Asia to meet local practitioners, find their indigenous traditions, and offer knowledge. These probably brief seminars brought valuable information that melded with the local customs.

In my business, Transcendence Design, I use only those few universal elements of Feng Shui that are harmonious with Vastu and that I have found to be effective. For example, both systems advocate light and fresh air in homes and offices. Both point out the negative effect of clutter and stagnation of energy. Likewise, ceiling beams are considered an oppressive, unhealthy influence in both traditions. Both systems speak of the importance of the front door and its being clean and in good repair, and that nothing in the household should remain in a broken state. In the bedroom, both systems see the intelligence of having space on both sides of the bed.

Feng Shui Compass School's *bagua*, an eight-sided diagram of the zones of a building or room, corresponds in some areas to Vastu, which aligns the built space with the cardinal directions. Career is influenced by the north in both Vastu and Feng Shui, and both perceive the southwest as the area for the master bedroom and relationships. Northwest is the area of movement in Vastu and travel in Feng Shui. Northeast is knowledge in Feng Shui and spiritual knowledge in Vastu. Other areas of the *bagua* do not correspond with Vastu's profound understanding of the effect of elemental energies. After careful study and practice, I see Vastu as offering much greater depth and benefit than Feng Shui.

Design and Architectural Styles

Vastu is not a style of architecture or interior design; it is a complete system based on natural laws that can work with your own sense of style and beauty. You can have a Tudor Vastu home or a New Mexico Territorial Vastu home, Spanish Mission-style Vastu architecture or log cabin Vastu architecture. Likewise, you are not restricted to a particular style of interior design: lots of frills and lace or a stark, Zen-inspired interior can both work within the Vastu framework. Almost all of your individual preferences in color, style, materials, texture, and furnishings can work in a Vastu home or office. There is a diverse range of possibilities within the Vastu guidelines for built spaces that are nurturing

Transparent, one of a kind, handpainted
silk curtain panels by artist Laura Trisiano
enhance the connection of this home
with nature.

and supportive "living organisms." Vastu is universal in its application and does not depend on fitting in with your personal taste. As long as it follows the guidelines, is beautiful, and is well-constructed with natural materials, any architectural style or design scheme can work with Vastu.

Applying Vastu Principles

When building according to Vastu, follow all details, precise measurements, and directional alignments specified by a Vastu architect. The result will be worth the meticulous attention. With an existing building, don't be feverish to make all the changes at once. Make changes and observe the results; notice how the space looks and feels. This will guide you to the next round of improvements and increase your sensitivity to what is happening inside of you and in your environment. Observe what is happening in the mind as well. If you feel a sense of frenetic urgency, slow down and get centered before taking action. On the other hand, don't put off improvements and their resulting benefits. Act with balance.

If your existing home or office does not comply with Vastu rules, take a deep breath, let go, and do what is possible. I keep finding ways to refine and improve my own home; it is an evolutionary process. Your environment and your inner experience can keep transmuting. As Zen Buddhist master Suzuki Roshi puts it, "Everything is already perfect, but there is always room for improvement." The ultimate improvement is building according to Vastu. If you work with a Vastu architect, you can plan a true dream house that can surpass your expectations. It will be a living organism that totally nourishes and supports you with a palpable feeling of life, peace, and vitality.

Section II

vastu basics

The principles of Vastu connect the dweller of the Vastu home with subtle laws of nature, such as the energy grid of the earth, beneficial earth energies, and cosmic energies from the sun. They also align the home with the five elements of earth, water, fire, air, and space. When applied to the construction of a new home, Vastu principles create a "living organism"; this true Vastu structure matches the resonance of the inhabitants, is totally in harmony with nature, and harnesses physics and sacred mathematics to do so. When we apply the basics of Vastu to existing structures, they become healthier, more supportive, and more in tune with nature. We humans are living Vastu structures, as are the earth and the universe. It only makes sense to construct buildings that do not disrupt that alignment with nature.

Section Two explains the elements of Vastu, including the grid pattern of the *Vastu Purusha Mandala*, the mother wall, the eight directions and the center, the five elements, and their effects. You will be able to use this information to increase your home's alignment with nature and its support. The importance of beauty, natural materials, and the effective use of color are also covered in this section.

Vastu Purusha Mandala

The basic design element of a Vastu building is the *Vastu Purusha Mandala*. It is also used for planning a community. Ganapati Sthapati and others describe the *Vastu Purusha Mandala* as "the diagram of the universe in miniature."[1] To understand that this is much more profound than just an orderly grid pattern, let's first look at the concept of the *mandala* and then of Purusha.

The word *mandala* in Sanskrit means "circle." A *mandala* is a type of sacred geometry or cosmic diagram, usually square or circular in form, that gives graphic representation of what exists on a more subtle level of reality than the one we usually perceive. Some Buddhist meditation techniques use *mandalas* as a meditation visualization device. Since mandalas are archetypal images, they are found throughout nature and art in many cultures around the world.

All *mandalas* have radial symmetry, which means that they radiate out from a center point in a balanced manner with the same or similarly structured components in all directions. This radial structure is directly related to the subtle mechanics of creation: unseen, unmanifest pure energy or pure consciousness enters the world of form through a central point and then radiates out as a physical manifestation. The following sections on concentric squares and the center in architecture explain this concept in greater depth.

Purusha is sometimes described as a mythological, ravenous being that had to be controlled by the gods, who ended up sitting on top of him to restrain and rehabilitate him. This is usually interpreted metaphorically in terms of creating effective order. Purusha is also frequently described as the archetypal Cosmic Man, an embodiment of pure consciousness. Purusha is the Universal Self, the transcendental principle of the Masculine Divine. He is contained face down in a square grid, representing his union with the Feminine Divine in her guise as Prakriti or Earth Mother, supporter of day-to-day human existence, "Nature" incarnate. Of course ultimately both cosmic and earth energies have the same essence and are beyond gender. On one level, the *Vastu Purusha Mandala* represents the harmonious union of masculine and feminine divine, of cosmic energies and earth energies. This union creates a lively, balanced wholeness and a home where the deepest level of Self is nestled within nature. As J. C. Cooper puts it in *An Illustrated Encyclopaedia of Traditional Symbols*, the house can be seen as "the sheltering aspect of the Great Mother." We all need this kind of home. Vastu, the yoga of design, offers us shelter with a fountain of joy from within, enlivened consciousness, and support of nature. The concrete basis for achieving these experiences is utilizing the potency of the *Vastu Purusha Mandala*. This requires a trained Vastu expert.

The *Vastu Purusha Mandala* is divided into a grid, usually with a minimum of nine sections representing the nine directions of north, south, east, west, northeast, northwest, southeast, southwest, and the center. Since buildings are three-dimensional, this is actually a cube, not a two-dimensional square. Purusha is contained within this cubic *mandala* with his head in the northeast, the most sacred sector. Usually his feet are together in the southwest, and his knees and elbows occupy the

Nineteenth-century seed syllable Tibetan Buddhist mandalas.

northwest and southeast. Thus Purusha, representing consciousness, fills up the earthly space of the diagram. The torso and main organs of the body are primarily in the center sector of the grid pattern, which is kept open and clear.

There are special energy and power points in this area that are called *marma* points. Both the human body and the body of Vastu Purusha within each built space have *marmas*. *Marma* in Sanskrit means something secret, mysterious, and not well understood, according to Ayurvedic doctor Vaidya R. K. Mishra. *Marma* also means "hidden" and "vital." Through the use of Ayurvedic acupressure, imbalances in the body can be removed and the flow of pranic energy restored. *Marma* points on the body of Vastu Purusha are important for maintenance of the health of an architectural space. A few guidelines are given in the upcoming section on the center direction.

There are thirty-two different patterns of the *Vastu Purusha Mandala*, ranging from a single undivided square of 1 x 1 up to a grid pattern of 32 x 32 = 1024 sections. The two most important

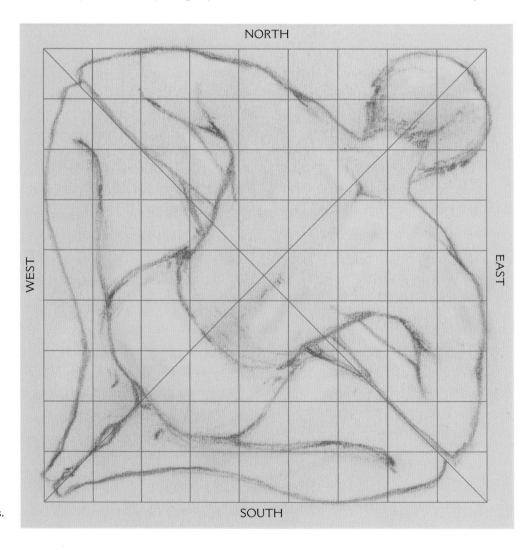

Vastu Purusha Mandala for homes.

and frequently used have 8 x 8 = 64 and 9 x 9 = 81 grid sections. The 9 x 9 energy grid pattern often is made up of rectangular rather than square modules, or *padas*. Each grid section or *pada* is occupied on the subtle level by a particular *deva*, or impulse of creative intelligence in nature, that has jurisdiction over some aspect of life.

The 8 x 8 grid pattern is the *Manduka* (or *Manduka Pada*) *Vaastu Mandala*, which is used for temples. *Manduka* means "frog" in Sanskrit; *pada* in this instance means "spaces within the grid pattern." The traditional explanation does have to do with the way a frog moves: the grid pattern in *Manduka Pada* is considered to expand in jumps, representing the flow of the Unmanifest into the material plane to create the living organism of a temple. This corresponds on a small scale to the way the universe grows in the same way from its center point.[2]

The 9 x 9 grid pattern is called *Paramasayika Vaastu Mandala*; it is the grid pattern most frequently used for homes and other buildings that are not temples. The image on the facing page shows the *Vastu Purusha Mandala* in its 9 x 9 form with Purusha contained within the grid pattern of concentric squares. *Paramasayika* is the livable architectural pattern that best holds the subtle energies in the physical plane that we exist and flourish in. The grid pattern is not an arbitrary or simply convenient drawing tool; it is a description of the subtle means of creation and manifestation. Another factor to remember is that, although the *Vastu Purusha Mandala* is described here as a two-dimensional square, it is actually a three-dimensional cube, as is the architectural space created from it.

Remember that Vastu is scientifically based and utilizes the subtle mechanics of creation to transform energy into matter in a harmonious way. Sthapati refers to the *Vastu Purusha Mandala* as "the unified field of energy and matter," which again reminds us of Einstein's famous realization of the equivalence of energy and matter. Another revered writer on Indian architecture, Stella Kramrisch, says the *Vastu Purusha Mandala* depicts "divine essence becoming form."[3] She explains, "Purusha is the universal Essence . . . whence all originates . . . In bodily existence, Purusha, the essence, becomes the Form."[4]

concentric squares

The concentric squares of the *Vastu Purusha Mandala* are an archetypal pattern that establishes a potent, healthy, energetic effect. Square concentricities are found in many world cultures. This square grid form is called *Sarvatobhadra* in Sanskrit. It is the fundamental structure of innumerable temples and works of art created by architects and artists around the world, both consciously and unconsciously: a series of concentric squares that infinitely recede to the unseen center of the universe from which all the manifestations and creations of our world emerge. Likewise, they can be viewed as an expansion of the infinite point out into the relative, physical world. This pattern is common in the architecture of Egypt, the Americas, Europe, and various parts of Asia. Pagodas in

PAISACHIKA PADA								
MANUSHA PADA								
DEIVIKA PADA								
BRAHMA PADA								

Vastu Purusha Mandala **showing the concentric zones of energy.**

Southeast and East Asia and the Step Pyramid at Saqara, Egypt are familiar examples of these concentric squares in architecture.

The diagram on this page depicts the four concentric belts of energy in the *Vastu Purusha Mandala* and, according to Mayan, in the earth itself. The central core is the *Brahma Pada*, the highly charged zone of primal source energy, sometimes referred to as a "hot zone." Around that is a band known as *Deivika Pada*, or "luminous space." The next outwardly expanding zone is *Manusha Pada*, or "conscious space." The outermost band is *Paisachika Pada*, or "gross material space."[5] The innermost two concentric squares are zones that should be free and open, with no walls or heavy items. The other two are for human habitation and physical structure.

padas and pada devatas

The Sanskrit term *pada* means "foot," "measure," or section of the energy grid pattern in the *Vastu Purusha Mandala*. These are important since each section has its own particular properties which, when properly honored, are more supportive of fulfilling our desires for peace, prosperity, health, and happiness. Each *pada* houses a particular *devata*, or impulse of creative intelligence in nature. These *pada devatas* are specific and have names. Just as people have different roles and duties in various areas of life, so do *pada devatas*. They deal with aspects of the five elements, such as air and water, and with cosmic energies, such as forms of the divine and the life-supporting energies of the sun. The effect of *pada devatas* is discussed in regard to positioning the home's entrance in Section Three.

The Mother Wall

The mother wall of the building is the outer boundary of the square or rectangular *Vastu Purusha Mandala*. It is one of Vastu's chief guidelines for creating a living organism; without it, you can end up with a dead or sick building. Properly placed extensions can be added to it when designed according to the grid pattern of the *Vastu Purusha Mandala*.

Square and rectangular buildings have a symmetry that can be quite beautiful, but you are not limited to that shape. It is not a straitjacket. Linear or curved extensions can always be added to the design for aesthetics and function, so long as they are modulated on the grid pattern. Bathrooms and staircases are ideal in these extensions from the mother wall. Most architecture does not take the mother wall and appropriately applied extensions into account. This creates energetic problems that plague the buildings' occupants, since it breaks the resonant connection with the laws of nature. More information on extensions is discussed later in this section.

This home benefits from the healthy resonance of its all natural, hand-crafted building materials: clay-straw, wood, and paper shoji screens. The flowers in a ceramic vase add another connection with the beauty and *prana* of nature.

The Eight Directions and the Center

Vastu takes into consideration nine main directions: the four cardinal directions of north, south, east, and west; the intermediate directions of northeast, northwest, southeast, and southwest; and the centermost point from which energy and *prana* pour forth. The eight directions and the center are a motif in other world traditions, including Navajo sand painting, Tibetan Buddhist sand *mandalas,* and the art of Indonesia and Malaysia.

The formulators of Vastu perceived the effect of the directions on human life. Proper orientation with the cardinal directions aligns the built space with the energy grid of the earth and brings great harmonious benefit; it allows the home to properly absorb energy flowing from the sun, moon, stars, and the earth itself.

Each of the nine directions (north, northeast, east, southeast, south, southwest, west, northwest, and the center) is important and has specific elements associated with it. *Prana* and energy pour forth from the center (and from outside of the built space as well) through directional lines, which are called *yonis,* or "lifelines." *Yoni* is a Sanskrit term that also refers to female genitals; in this context it indicates that when building according to Vastu guidelines, the new home or other building is a living organism that is being nourished and birthed.

north, south, east, and west

East is the most auspicious direction, since this is where the life-sustaining light of the sun rises each day. You have probably noticed how uplifted you feel and how sparkly your home becomes on those spring days when the morning sun shines brightly and illuminates a home that has been colder and darker through the long winter months—you feel more hopeful and inspired, as if you have come to life again. The sun's light, warmth, and energy are vital and have a profound effect upon us. The early morning's gentle ultraviolet is healing and needed by your body for optimal health. You can enhance your sense of well-being by sunbathing for a brief period of ten to thirty minutes in the early morning. If you have done this, you already know how pleasurable and relaxing it is: the early morning rays of the sun feel like they are caressing your skin instead of attacking it. Clearly the east side of the house should have openings to bring the eastern energy of the sun into the home. An east entrance to a home can improve health and is also ideal for a medical facility.

North and east provide nourishing cosmic energies, so there should be more unobstructed open space on your lot in these directions, and more windows and doors to let in these supportive energies. The north is the area of wealth, health, and career. The ground of your lot should either be level or it should be higher in the south and west and lower in the north and east, so that the subtle

The essential fact of architecture and, indeed, of human life on earth [is] the relation of mankind to the natural order.

—Architect Vincent Scully

This serene earth-toned southwest bedroom benefits from the shelter of tall trees.

energies from the north and east can collect and enter the home. If you need to, you can build up the south or west to create a better situation energetically.

Heavy furnishings should be mainly in the south and west; for the same reason, your home or office can have more floors in the south and west, thus adding more weight. Keep the north and east more open with lighter objects. Since there will be fewer furnishings in the north and east, you can have more of your indoor traffic patterns there.

To protect yourself and the interior of your space from intense and harsh rays coming from the west and south, walls are sometimes incorrectly prescribed to be thicker and higher in these directions, but this is a misinterpretation of Vastu knowledge.

On the *Vastu Purusha Mandala* grid there are at least two acceptable segments of the nine that face in every one of the four directions that can be used for your front door, so there is nothing inherently wrong with a south- or west-facing front door, so long as it is properly placed. This information will be covered in Section Three of this book. If your front door is in the south or west, you might want to add a protective portico to protect from intense heat and sun.

Since there are frequently lots of south and west windows in an existing home, you can help balance this by having windows on the opposite side (north or east) as well, which is advised in Vastu anyway. A fountain or other water feature to the north of the home provides some energetic counterbalance for an open south side of the home, thus improving health and finances. Anyone who has ever had a south-facing desk next to a window knows what a weakening influence intense direct glare has on their eyes and energy. Ideally you will have tall trees in the south and west. If this is not the case, window film is especially practical in sunny areas that have large windows for sunset views. You do not need UV window film on east and north windows; there are beneficial, gentle cosmic rays radiating from the east and north that you want to welcome into your home. You can also have window film installed in your car's windows as a health and safety factor to help cut glare and protect your skin. Today's UV film cuts solar heat transmission and harmful infrared rays coming through glass and deflects ninety-nine percent of ultraviolet rays, providing a modern technological solution to an age-old problem. You can see clearly, save on energy bills, and protect delicate fabrics and colors. Some window films utilize particles of silver, a precious metal that has a cooling effect.

northeast, northwest, southeast, southwest

The intermediate directions of northeast, southeast, southwest, and northwest have benefits that can be harnessed when they are able to collect in the corners of the building. Designing a structure that faces these intermediate directions creates a disruptive effect. Unfortunately, many buildings are sited this way out of ignorance.

The directions of northeast and southwest, which are on a diagonal in the *Vastu Purusha Mandala* from the top of Purusha's head to the tip of his feet, are considered sacred. The northeast is the area for knowledge, meditation rooms, spiritual altars and practices, and the best place to keep medi-

Seven Sources of *Prana*

1. An open window in the northwest, the quadrant where the air element is predominant

2. A *vamsa danda*, or spine of light, running unobstructed from the front door straight through the house to a back window or door

3. An open *Brahmasthan* to allow the structure to generate *prana* from the middle of the house

4. Live plants and flowers in the house and gardens

5. Meditation and healing breath techniques like Sudarshan Kriya

6. Fresh, organic foods

7. Water elements like the ocean, mountain streams with waterfalls, and fountains that replicate these places in our homes

cines for increased potency. Clean, well-maintained swimming pools, ponds, fountains, waterfalls, hot tubs, and aquariums give the best effect when they are placed in the northeast. A client's wife who was skeptical about Vastu admitted that projects went more smoothly after they installed a waterfall and pond in the northeast sector of their suburban Chicago yard.

Do not place the bathroom or kitchen in the northeast. If they are already there and you cannot renovate, there are *yantra* rectifications you can utilize to help partially alleviate the negative effect. *Yantras* are sacred geometrical patterns that generate a positive influence; they are discussed in detail in Section Four.

Also be mindful of where you place the hamper for dirty clothes and your trash cans in rooms. If they are in the northeast, move them. The northeast should be kept as clean, pure, and open as possible.

The northwest is the best spot for guest rooms; businesses should place goods that are for sale in this area. These guidelines are dictated by the elemental energies that are predominant in the various directions; the following material on the five elements gives greater understanding of appropriate placement with the directions. More details on the directions follow in the information about the five elements and color and in Section Three.

the center

The center of the *Vastu Purusha Mandala* is called the *Brahmasthan*. It is the interface between the seen and the unseen, the manifest and unmanifest. Rina Swintzell describes the equivalent in Southwest Pueblo culture: "The Tewa word for plaza is *bupingeh*, which translates into English as the 'center [middle] heart place.'"[6] We know immediately that this must be about something spiritual in nature, since it is the heart. It allows cosmic breath to enter the community and connect people with universal energies.

The center of the building should be kept clean and clear, a revered open space. If it is practical, an atrium or courtyard left open to the sky is ideal, since this brings some fresh, cooling influence to this energetically intense zone. You do not have to avoid use of this area, but it shouldn't be actively used on an everyday basis or contain large, heavy objects.

Panchabhutas: The Five Elements

Vastu reestablishes a missing connection between people and the rest of the world of nature. The five elements of creation, known as the *panchabhutas,* are honored and balanced. This level of alignment with nature enhances the flow of *prana*, universal life-force energy, within a home or other building. Honoring nature is always sacred. It's clear that respect and care of our natural environment is a divine contract. We have all seen the result of ignoring this wisdom.

The bindu obtained in the centre is the life-breath of the earth.

——Chapter 2, Verse 14 of *Vastu Sutra Upanishad*

There is a shining point where all lines intersect.

——Bill Moyers' Summary of Black Elk

The five elements in the Vedic system are space, air, fire, water, and earth. Space is the most subtle of the five elements; earth is the densest. It is traditionally understood from *Taitiriya Upanishad* that each element emerges in turn from the previous, less dense element, which is how material form develops out of unmanifest space.

Each of these five basic elements is energetically associated with a particular direction. This is not an arbitrary assignment but an acknowledgement of subtle laws of nature. These more concentrated, specialized energies are predominant in different specific sectors of the *Vastu Purusha Mandala*. By honoring the various elements and their primal energies, we are in greater harmony with nature. This results in greater harmony and ease in our lives.

earth: *bhumi* or *prithivi*

The earth element is associated with the southwest direction, the best choice for the location for the master bedroom. Earth is a solid, dense, and grounded element. We all need a physical basis or foundation to survive in this world. Plants, trees, soil, rocks, and mountains represent the earth element.

water: *jala*

Northeast is the direction where the energy waves of the water element collect. This makes it the best placement for indoor and outdoor water features: swimming pools, fountains, ponds, waterfalls, and aquariums. Water is frequently used as a metaphor for pure consciousness in the Vedic tradition.

fire: *agni*

The fire element is predominant in the southeast, so it is the best placement for kitchens, fireplaces, computers, and other electrical equipment. Digestion in the body and transformation are also the realm of *Agni*. To add and honor this element, light fires! Enjoy an indoor or outdoor fireplace in the southeast, and light candles (preferably those made of beeswax, since it is healthier and natural, whereas paraffin candles and lead wicks are toxic).

air: *vayu*

The air element is liveliest in the northwest, so put fans, wind streamers, mobiles, wind chimes, and air purifiers here. Use your aesthetic sense and do not add anything meaningless or overdone. The concept of movement in general is associated with this element and its direction. To reap the benefits of the *prana* in the air, learn and practice *pranayama* breathing techniques, preferably with

Buddha with waterfall, fresco painting, Karla Refojo.

windows open enough to bring fresh air into the room. Be sure that the air in your home is fresh. If your home has stagnant areas, you can use fans to keep the air moving.

space: *akasha*

This element is directly linked to sound and silence. It is sometimes called "ether," but this isn't the kind of ether that puts you to sleep. *Akasha* is the expansiveness in the center of the architectural form and in the center of each room, the element of "energetic and dynamic space."[7] The center of the building and each room is called the *Brahmasthan*; honor it in each area by keeping it clean and open. Don't put heavy objects here.

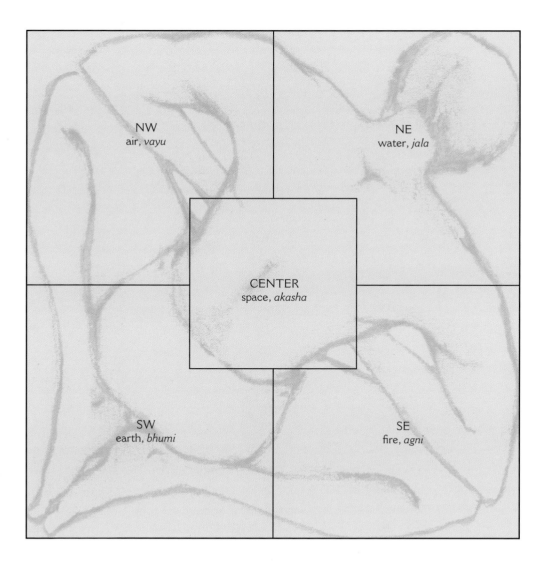

NW
air, *vayu*

NE
water, *jala*

CENTER
space, *akasha*

SW
earth, *bhumi*

SE
fire, *agni*

Additions, Extensions, and Missing Corners

Although your home does not need to be a simple square or rectangle, irregularly shaped buildings and rooms can create problems for their inhabitants. If an area is missing or cut off, you lose the balancing effect of that element of nature and its characteristic influences. One personal experience of this was a house I rented that was missing its northwest corner and therefore disrupted the air element. I was unable to settle down in this home, and less than a year later the landlord wanted the house back for himself. Since the house looked and felt so much better from my application of Vastu, it became more desirable to the landlord. Friends put a positive spin on this, saying it proves that Vastu really works. I ended up benefiting from the situation, since I was propelled by nature into an even more suitable home with a more beautiful setting.

Northeast extensions to your home are considered auspicious, since they enhance that direction's beneficial energy. Missing areas increase difficulties for those dwelling in the built space, since this means that the elemental energies would be weakened. Cutting off the corners also has a negative effect since it eliminates the strongest concentration of the elemental energies. Unfortunately, this is the situation in many residential buildings, due to ignorance of this law of nature. One potent solution is to put a line of bricks, stones, or tiles on the ground to complete the missing mother wall of the house. If it is absolutely not possible to remodel with the aid of a Vastu architect, another approach is appeasement of the missing energy to soften the effect. The Vedic tradition's potent sacred geometry, described in Section Four, is an aid here. Place the corresponding *yantra* in the interior area closest to the missing corner. You can also follow artist Bill Witherspoon's lead, as documented in his unpublished paper "Art and Technology." Bury the yantra in the ground in the "missing" area. It will generate a beneficial energetic field to help compensate for the missing element. In the case of a missing chunk of the northwest corner, the influence of the air element and the moon need support. Use of a moon yantra will help with emotions that could be challenged because of this missing northwest area, since the moon is its planetary lord. A wind ornament, wind chime, or mobile to honor the air element could go in the missing area, which will be outside the home in the yard. This honors the element but does not correct the Vastu defect.

Similar things can be done if your home or office is missing any of the other three corners: For a missing southwest corner, place heavy rocks or plant trees to add weight and to honor the earth element. The yantra to affix on the wall and bury in the ground in this case is the yantra for Rahu. For a missing southeast corner, add a fire element, such as a fire pit or candles, and bury a Venus yantra. For a missing northeast corner, install a water feature in the yard—fountain, waterfall, or pond—and bury Jupiter and Ketu yantras. Also bury or affix to the wall the Sri Yantra, the most powerful of all yantras.

I go to Nature to be soothed and healed, and to have my senses put in tune once more.

—JOHN BURROUGHS

Nature's laws affirm instead of prohibiting. If you violate her laws you are your own prosecuting attorney, judge, [and] jury.

—LUTHER BURBANK

As far as we know, Vastu traditionally expected people as a matter of course to follow its sacred guidelines and build correctly the first time—and not build additions later without careful attention to precise guidelines, since it would change the flow of *prana* within the home. This is not how the vast majority of homes and other buildings are designed today, so we have to take steps to compensate for design errors that produce negative effects. There are rectifications that can help a home with poor Vastu, as described above, but if you need to remodel or add on to a house, make the desired changes with someone professionally trained in Vastu, so that the right dimensions and shapes are reestablished with precision on the grid lines of the *Vastu Purusha Mandala*.

Leave It to Nature, pastels and oil pastels on paper, Sherri Silverman.

Natural Materials

The use of natural materials—tile, stone, true adobe, brick, natural linoleum, bamboo, wood—enhances the health and energy of a space and the people who dwell there. Avoid synthetic materials. Many of the plastics we use release dangerous substances into the air for years and create a toxic interior environment. Metals like steel and iron, although manufactured from elements in the earth, can create or aggravate electromagnetic disturbances in buildings by reacting with electrical wiring and blocking beneficial energies. Vaidya R. K. Mishra, a great expert in Ayurveda, refers to *Indrabajraabhi Dagdha*, electromagnetic vibrational toxicity, as one of the most serious threats to health. We are bombarded with electromagnetic toxins from power lines, electrical wiring in buildings, steel structures (which magnify and disrupt energetic fields) and other man-made sources.

The earth naturally gives off both beneficial and harmful radiations. One of its positive radiations is geomagnetic. Before chemical/industrial pollution and man-made electrical fields, being close to the earth provided a great deal of support for human health. Concrete and steel, which are used extensively in construction, disrupt these earth energies. Metal bed frames and electrical fields from clocks plugged into electrical outlets also interfere with our connection with the natural, nourishing geomagnetism of the earth. Choose wood, rattan, or another natural material for your bed frame.

A beautiful effect is created when locally found, natural building materials are used in the structure of a home. One of the advantages of this, in addition to convenience and ease of transportation, is that it creates a unified wholeness between the house and its natural environment. This corresponds directly to Vastu's underlying principle of being in harmony with nature.

Natural fibers like cotton, silk, wool, hemp, flax, beechwood cellulose, and linen are healthy and breathable. Silk is also protective energetically. Natural rubber made from the sap of the *Hevea brasiliensis* tree has antibacterial properties. Silk, natural rubber, and wool have superior moisture wicking properties, so they are excellent for mattresses, pillows, and other bedding. These natural materials limit dust mites and prevent allergic reactions. If you want wall-to-wall carpeting, select natural fibers with no chemical treatments. Area rugs can be silk, cotton, flax, wool, or other natural

The starburst of this exquisite eco-friendly table is made from eighty-year-old palm trees that are past their years of producing coconuts. Sustainable walnut and tree sap complete the Pava Bistro table from environmental language, available through Transcendence Design.

Above: Handmade ceramic tiles by artist Chris Gryder are a way to embellish your home with natural materials and subject matter.

Opposite: This charming Santa Fe bathroom has beautiful walls created with American Clay earth plasters.

It is alarming that publications devoted to architecture have banished from their pages the words Beauty, Inspiration, Magic, Spellbound, Enchantment, as well as the concepts of Serenity, Silence, Intimacy, and Amazement. All these have nestled in my soul.

—MEXICAN ARCHITECT LUIS BARRAGÁN

materials. Check that the glue and backing are also natural materials that do not off-gas. Chemical-free carpet pads made of jute and goat hair are a good choice.

Traditionally, Vastu recommends the use of certain stones in your home and avoidance of others. Granite, slate, and limestone are all fine. Vastu elicits the value of a piece of stone in an intriguing way. If it has a musical ring when struck, it is considered usable. If the sound is more of a thud, the material is not acceptable. Marble is not usually used since it is considered to be unmusical. *Mayamata* suggests that bricks also have a harmonious or pleasing sound to them. Stone is a good choice for a home's foundation but not for all its wall surfaces, since overuse of stone can create a cold, hard effect.

In general, Vastu is in agreement with much of green architecture, sustainable building, and Baubiologie. Building a Vastu structure enables you to actually improve the environment by means of the vibrational effect generated by a Vastu structure. Use fresh, new materials that do not carry the vibrations of previous users. Some of this effect is observable. If the materials seem to carry a heavy, murky, "unclean," or unpleasant energy, don't use them.

You will improve your health if you get rid of cleaning and laundry supplies with dangerous chemicals and artificial ingredients and switch to non-toxic, natural household cleaners. Studies have shown that essential oils (which are frequently in non-toxic cleaners) are more effective against bacteria, viruses, fungus, and mold than chemicals and antibiotics. Your house will smell better and be less toxic. This protects the earth's soil and water from further contamination. You can make a conscious choice not to use chemical cleaners, since they create an extra burden on water treatment facilities and cannot be easily removed.

When choosing paint and varnish, do not select the conventional products that off-gas and create illness. Use no-VOC paints, natural paints, and clay-based natural earth plaster created with earth pigments. These can be applied over existing gypsum drywall or Sheetrock to create healthier and more beautiful interior walls.

Sundari: Beauty

Luis Barragán's excellent choice of words to describe the energy and physical form of architecture is well in accord with Vastu. Aesthetics are a major consideration: the site and the building must be pleasing in its form and effect. All levels of life should be nourished in architecture: physical protection, emotional well-being, sensory satisfaction.

Go by all the rules but neglect to create a beautiful building, and it is not fully Vastu. This is evident in the Vastu texts that describe the creation of the world. Here is an apt excerpt from the *Shilpa Vidya Rahasyopanisad*: "The space became decorated and beautified with stars and other luminous bodies. The Earth also became studded and decorated with mountains, forests, trees

and so forth." Vastu encourages you to imitate nature and divine creation by beautifying your own spaces. This is a delightful concept: adorning your world with beauty makes your life more in harmony with nature.

Hearing beautiful sounds heals the ears. Seeing beauty heals the eyes. As writer Alice Walker puts it,

> *Whenever you are*
> *creating beauty*
> *around you,*
> *you are restoring*
> *your own soul.*

Decorating is not just a matter of accumulating stuff; you should adorn your home with beauty that nourishes your soul. Choose your furnishings carefully and get rid of anything you don't like or that is worn out. Only add items if you find them useful, beautiful, and comfortable. Adding ornamentation is an act of honoring. Ananda Coomaraswamy wrote, "The beauty of anything unadorned is not increased by ornament, but made more effective by it . . . It is generally by means of what we now call its decoration that a thing is ritually transformed and made to function spiritually as well as physically."[8]

Remember that true Vastu requires all levels to be fulfilled: functional space, aesthetics, spiritual energy, and upliftment for your soul. As Ajit Mookerjee and Madhu Khanna wrote in *The Tantric Way*, "The beautiful and the spiritual form an inseparable whole. Beauty is a symbol of the divine."[9] The beauty we perceive with our senses is illuminated by the underlying radiance of the Absolute, the formless source of all existence and forms, which shines through the objects of this material world. Since Vastu is a spiritually based science, its foundation is this unbounded field of pure consciousness and eternal beauty.

May Sundari, that aspect of the Goddess who personifies beauty, enlighten your life, your home, and your workspace!

Rasa: Aesthetic Juice

The beauty emanating from this artfully arranged setting demonstrates how *sundari* attracts our attention. We are instinctively drawn to beauty and know that it nourishes our lives.

Great appreciation of beauty is a reflection of the beauty of your own inner nature. India scholar David Frawley writes, "Sundari shoots us with the arrows of delight, revealing all the forms of creation as aspects of our own blissful nature of pure consciousness."[10] Radiant works of art evoke in the refined viewer *rasavadana*, aesthetic experience. Indian aesthetics traditionally defines beauty in terms of the effectiveness of the emotional impact of works of art, which

> Through the beauty of material things we come to understand God.
>
> —ABBOT SUGER OF ST. DENIS, FOUNDER OF THE GOTHIC STYLE OF SACRED ARCHITECTURE

include architectural spaces and interior design; beauty is described in terms of *rasa*. *Rasa* is a Sanskrit term that translates as the juice or sap of a plant. In its use as a basic component of what is pleasing in the arts, architecture, and design, *rasa* refers to the juice or emotional flavor evoked by the experience of art. If something is juicy, it is full of that magical life-force energy that helps create the transcendental home.

Traditionally there are nine major *rasas*, which are enumerated in the *Vastu Sutra Upanishad*. Some *rasas* are appropriate for your home or office; some are not. Clearly, *rasas* of *Shanta* (peace, tranquility, serenity), *Hasya* (laughter, playfulness, good-natured humor), *Vira* (heroism), the uplifting aspects of *Adbhuta* (celestial joy, astonishment at the marvelous), and *Shringara* (romance, healthy eroticism, the blissful sweetness of love) can be appropriate for different zones of your home. The desire for serenity explains why so many people like to have Buddha statues in their homes, gardens, and offices. If you are evoking *Shringara rasa* in your home, make it the aspect of happy, united couples rather than the anguish of separation. *Karuna* (compassion), *Raudra* (anger, fury), *Bhayanaka* (fear), *Bibhatsa* (the odious), and other evocations of sorrow, despair, deprivation, anxiety, and disgust may be powerfully expressed through the arts but are not healing, nourishing influences in your home or office, unless they show the overcoming of these obstacles in an inspirational manner. What you put your attention on grows stronger in your life; you can choose between focusing on and increasing sadness, depression, and misery in your life, or you can make choices that help you become more established in peace and happiness.

A *rasika* is someone who is sensitive enough to be moved profoundly by and have a transcendent experience from observing an exquisite work of art. The aesthetic experience touches so deeply as to integrate experience of many different levels of existence, thus creating what becomes a spiritual experience. Artwork and home design that elicit this wholeness are beautiful and truly representative of what Vastu offers to our lives.

> An idea that seemed to me to be of use to everyone—whether you think about it consciously or not—the idea of filling a space in a beautiful way.
>
> —Georgia O'Keeffe

Color

Color has a powerful, emotional impact that is direct and personal. Each shade of a color has a distinct vibrational rate that deeply affects us energetically. There are nourishing shades of all colors. Avoid those that feel depressing, harsh, painful, or jarring. Trust your own response in finding beautiful, pleasing colors. Get small paint samples to try on your walls and then observe the color at different times of the day, since changing sunlight and artificial lighting can make colors look quite different.

In addition to wall colors, you can bring color and its vitality into your home or business space with live plants, cut flowers and leaves, and other elements of nature that appeal to you. Wearing color as makeup, jewelry, and clothing is another healing way to nourish yourself. Colors are food for your well-being.

Although there are symbolic, culturally specific meanings for colors, there are also universal qualities of color and its effects. The following sections discuss color and the rainbow, *chakras*, Ayurveda, gemstones, the planets, and the five elements, followed by how to make color choices based on this information in conjunction with your own preferences and needs.

rainbow and *chakra* colors

The seven main colors in a rainbow are red, orange, yellow, green, blue, indigo, and violet. They correspond to some interpretations of the subtle energy *chakra* system in the human body, starting with red at the base *chakra* and moving through the range of colors to violet at the crown *chakra*.

RED is bold and full of zest, rarely subtle. Red immediately conveys a rich warmth and active, vital passion for life and existence. Spanish poet Rafael Alberti's "The apple's full flush in the round" evokes the somewhat blatant quality of red.

Red is the color associated with the first chakra, *Muladhara*, which is also called the root or base chakra, since it deals with the basic life issue of existence and survival. The feminine divine is represented by the color red in Tantric art, the masculine divine by the color white.

Egyptian Goddess: Sekhmet, pastels on paper, Sherri Silverman.

The solid vibrancy of ORANGE enlivens and energizes spaces and the people in them. Intensely colored orange foods—pumpkin, winter squashes, papaya, mango—are high in *prana* and thus feed our life-force. Orange is another color found in the flames of a fire. It represents the second chakra, *Svadishthana*, the area of sexuality, procreation, and creative energies.

BMoCA #4: Who are you? Where are you going? What have you contributed to this world?, pastels and pencil on paper, Sherri Silverman.

The right shades of YELLOW are uplifting like a sunny disposition. Yellows enhance mental processes, intellect, and creativity. The radiance of gold is yellow. The third chakra of our bodies, *Manipura*, found at the solar plexus a little above the navel, is yellow like the sun.

BMoCA #17: Light of the Divine, Golden Goddess, pastels and pencil on paper, Sherri Silverman.

GREEN is soothing and healing, symbolic of growth and life. Green suggests moisture and lush plant life.

Go deep within Me and then you'll know You.
Go deep within Forest fir pineleaf stemgreen
Go deep into Me and find the Unseen.
Go deep within Me and then you'll know you.

Go deep and explore
chartreuse limeleaf
deepest iridescent green
air-and-water seafoam lace
waves of delicate serene
Go deep into Me and find the Unseen.[11]

A chartreuse green, which contains some yellow, is also associated with the sprouting of creative energy. Years ago, I attended a wonderful poetry reading at Harvard University. All I remember now is my experience of the poet radiating a fresh chartreuse green aura while performing his poems. The experience of color remains, but the words dissolved.

Anahata, the heart chakra in the center of the chest, is considered green in color. May your heart open, sending forth sprouts of new life!

Fresh Sprouting, pastels on paper, Sherri Silverman.

BLUES are cooling. Blue can be a spiritual color suggesting and symbolizing the Absolute, "unbounded like the endless canopy of the sky," according to a Sanskrit expression. Painter Wassily Kandinsky wrote in his book *On the Spiritual in Art*, "The deeper the blue, the more it summons man into infinity and awakens in him the desire for the absolute."

In India, the color blue is frequently associated with the beloved Krishna, since as a metaphor for the divine, he is associated with the vast, infinite sky. The following is a poem I've written about Krishna:

I carry Home within me
I beautify it and adorn it
With flowers and with jewels

Those who know the House do the same

Lapis is not so dark as he who dwells there
His skies expand within me
They cradle me as I house it all [12]

Blue is also the color of the throat of Shiva, the transformer, due to a powerful poison he swallowed and held there in order to save others from its effect. The throat chakra, *Visuddha*, is blue in color.

Too much blue in the wrong shades can lead to depression. It's all (and always) a matter of balance.

The blue-purple of INDIGO is deep, cool, and calming. Think "mood indigo." It helps you settle into your inner Self, what poet T. S. Eliot called in his poem "Burnt Norton," "the still point of the turning world." This is perceived through the third eye, the subtle inner vision of the meditative space of the sixth chakra, *Ajna*, located between the eyebrows.

Indigo Source,
pastels on paper,
Sherri Silverman.

VIOLET is generally a delicate, soothing, healing, spiritual color. It represents religious sanctity in many world traditions as well as royalty. Violet is the color associated with *Sahasrara*, the seventh or crown chakra of the body, the radiance of bliss consciousness.

Matthew in Violet,
pastels on paper,
Sherri Silverman.

color and ayurveda

Ayurveda, which in Sanskrit means "science or spiritual knowledge of life," is recognized as an excellent system to maintain and restore health and balance. Certain colors are considered most harmonious and healing for the three *doshas* (bio-forces or bodily constitutions) described by Ayurveda: *vata*, *pitta*, and *kapha*. Everyone has an individual bodily constitution which is either *vata*, *pitta*, *kapha*, or a combination type. *Doshas* are formed by interaction of the five elements: earth, water, fire, air, and space. There are many online tests to determine your *doshas*. Some contemporary Vastu books focus on an Ayurvedic approach to Vastu rectification; I recommend paying attention to this factor when choosing colors. In general, *vatas* need soothing and steadying; *pittas* need cooling; and *kaphas* need sparking into greater activity. If you have a dual-*dosha* constitution, pay attention to the colors for both *doshas*, keeping in mind the effect of seasonal weather.

For someone with a lot of *pitta*, a red room would be aggravating to the *pitta* tendency toward overheating and anger. *Pitta* people who love red can use small accents of the color, but they will be healthiest with cooling colors predominating in their homes and offices. The same red that is too hot for *pittas* could help a sluggish *kapha* feel more energized, alert, and motivated. *Kaphas* need more stimulating colors; soft pastels and cool colors will not have the right effect for them. People with a predominantly *vata* constitution need colors that are grounding and soothing. *Vatas* should choose colors that are not jarring to their nervous systems, which tend to get agitated, shaky, nervous, or anxious with too much stimulation. Pastels may work for some *vatas*, but if you find them insipid or too airy, choose deeper, richer, more grounding colors.

There are also particular colors that are connected to the nine directions and the five elements. Jyotish (Vedic astrology), another science related to Vastu, designates color associations for the planets. In addition, the planets are linked with different directions and types of rooms over which they have influence. These colors may be applied to your décor as the wall color, the main color of your furnishings, or accent colors. The transition from one room to another should be harmonious and pleasing, not jarring; when you look from one room into another, the juxtaposed colors of the two walls should be attractive to the eye.

color and the planets

There are nine influential celestial bodies, or *grahas*, in the Vedic astrological system of Jyotish: the sun (*Surya*), moon (*Chandra*), Mars (*Mangal*), Mercury (*Budha*), Jupiter (*Guru*), Venus (*Shukra*), Saturn (*Shani*), north/ascending lunar node (*Rahu*), and south/descending lunar node (*Ketu*). Neptune, Uranus, and Pluto are not part of the Vedic systems of astronomy and astrology. Color, its effect upon us, and the realms of nature and the cosmos are closely connected. These nine celestial luminaries, or *grahas,* are associated with colorful gemstones as well as directions.

In the following descriptions of *grahas* and their corresponding gemstones and colors, the Sanskrit for the *graha,* or celestial body, is followed by the English name, associated gemstones, colors, and direction. The colors corresponding to these planetary bodies can be used on the walls of your home or as decorative accents and art.

NW Moon	N Mercury	NE Jupiter Ketu
W Saturn		E Sun
SW Rahu	S Mars	SE Venus

Above: The celestial bodies that rule the directions.

Surya/Sun: ruby, garnet; red, orange, sunlight colors; east. If your east wall is blocked and windowless, create the effect of a sunlit room with paint. This is a great opportunity to use warm, sunny color. Yellows will work as well as the red-orange range here, since it is the color we most associate with being "sunny." Vastu does not advocate the use of a lot of red interior walls for homes, perhaps because it is so stimulating.

Chandra/Moon: pearl, moonstone; white and pearly white, silver-gray; northwest. Silver-leafed walls create a stunning northwest room that also acknowledges the air element that is predominant in the northwest. A client and I chose this for a Colorado holistic skin care spa located in the northwest quadrant; her spa feels elegant and soothing.

Mangal/Mars: oxblood red coral; orange and red; south. If the drama of this color is not too stimulating for you, it can add vibrancy to a wall or as an accent in rooms that do not need calming energy.

Budha/Mercury: emerald, green tourmaline, peridot, jade; greens; north. A green north wall or room enriches your home and life on many levels, as does the addition of healthy plants. Green soothes and heals, and it suggests abundant wealth. If the north or your house is blocked or your finances seem to be, use green paint to help improve the energy and its results in your life.

Guru/Jupiter: yellow sapphire, yellow topaz, citrine; primarily yellows and golden yellows, yellows with some brown or orange; northeast. Honoring the planetary lord of the directions can give you useful options to consider when determining paint colors. Golden colors can be a wonderful, enlivening choice for a northeast room that is dark or cold.

Shukra/Venus: diamond, white sapphire, clear zircon; white, multi-color, indigo, blue; southeast. I often recommend that southeast bedrooms, which are contraindicated in Vastu, be cooled down and supported by using a color that honors the planetary lord Venus, such as a beautiful blue.

Shani/Saturn: blue sapphire, amethyst; dark blue, cobalt blue, black, violet; west. A western room or wall painted a rich, dark blue like the depths of the ocean or a saturated purple adds a sense of grounded privacy and riches. Do not choose a murky, depressing shade that increases an oppressive feeling.

Rahu/north lunar node: hessonite garnet; shades of orange with a golden, brown, or red tint; southwest. These rich, jewel-toned colors associated with the planetary lord of the southwest give you additional ideas for colors that can work well with the earth element. Their grounded quality links you to the earth.

Ketu/south lunar node: chrysoberyl cat's eye; golden-, green-, and brown-yellows, like the gemstone; secondary northeast. In addition to the colors for Jupiter, the main planetary ruler of the northeast, you can use *Ketu*'s colors to acknowledge *Ketu*'s influence and have additional options for the northeast of your home.

David Frawley explains some useful points to consider about planetary color therapy in his *Ayurvedic Healing: A Comprehensive Guide*: "The green ray of the planet Mercury . . . possesses the greatest force of healing and harmonization." "White gives peace and purity. Blue gives peace and detachment. Gold gives discrimination." He recommends three of the planetary colors for nervous system color therapy: "green (Mercury) for stopping pain, gold (Jupiter) for strengthening the nerves, white (the moon) for calming hypersensitivity."[13]

color and the five elements

The five elements are a key component in Vastu's alignment with nature, so the colors associated with the elements are particularly noteworthy:

Earth. The earth element is predominant in the southwest. Earth's colors are of course earth tones associated with soil: brown, cinnamon, ochre, sienna, umber, sepia, etc. Most earth-colored pigments were originally literally earth; they were harvested from soil and rock.

Water. The northeast direction's color is blue. Blues and green-blues are associated with the cool element of water. Honor the northeast by using blue paint, actual water features, or images of water. If you do not want blue walls, use the colors associated with Jupiter or Ketu as planetary regents of the northeast.

Fire. Fire's flame colors of golden-yellow, red, and golden-orange, intense rather than pale, acknowledge and embody *Agni*, fire energies in the southeast. If it is pleasing, an apricot kitchen would be uplifting for cooking chores. You can also utilize fiery accents in other southeast rooms of your home.

Air. Air's colors are light and delicate silver and white; these colors resonate with the air element, which is predominant in the northwest. Using another approach, you can propitiate Kali, the goddess associated with the air element, if there are defects in your home or office in the northwest. You can place a Kali image or chant a Kali mantra. Other options are to dedicate to Kali something dark blue in color in the northwest or to do more *pranayama*, breathing practices.

Space. The expansiveness of space does not have a particular color assigned to it since it is so subtle an element. However, on a subtle level the center of the *Vastu Purusha Mandala*, which is where the element of *akasha* (space) is most lively in a building, is luminous and golden. Gold as a color is beautiful, precious, and radiant; it infers something spiritual, earthly, and eternal.

choosing colors

These different approaches to color selection give you choices to fit your own needs and preferences. I developed it because I personally do not feel right about Sthapati's recommendation of only using very light shades of yellow, green, pink, blue, and creamy white.

If you know your Jyotish astrological chart, you can use color to help alleviate weak planets by using their colors to strengthen and honor them in your home and business. You can also wear any of these recommended colors. Consider which elements are predominant in the directions. If you want to work with Ayurveda or you really respond to the colors mentioned in that section, use colors for the *doshas* of members of your household. You can also help improve the energy of your home with color by knowing what planet rules that direction or that type of room. For example, as I mentioned a few paragraphs back, if your bedroom is in the southeast, which is against Vastu guidelines, adding some blue color will soften the overheating effect of the fire element and honor the ruling planet, Venus (although the best solution is to move the bedroom out of the southeast, preferably to the southwest).

Ayadi: Calculations to Fit the Individual

Ayadi gananam are mathematical calculations used to design a home, furnishings, jewelry, sculpture, or other items, according to proportions that fit the individual. The result for the lucky client is "to experience spiritual growth and enjoy spiritual peace and bliss at heart."[14] *Ayadi* calculations have six main components that all must be examined and found auspicious for the set of specific measurements to be favorable and supportive. This is a detailed analysis that must be performed by someone with the proper Vastu training. If you are building with a Vastu architect, make sure he or she knows this important aspect of Vastu. Most do the *Ayadi* calculations twice to make sure they are accurate. In-depth professional training is necessary to learn how to utilize and calculate Ayadi.

The word *Ayadi* has a wealth of meanings that it showers on the lucky person who has access to this long-hidden secret knowledge, including connection to wealth, energy, blissful harmony, and spiritual and cosmic origin. This esoteric knowledge contains a list of specific sizes that are known to be totally in accord with individual and cosmic energies. It does not include every size you might think of, but there are enough of them that your Vastu consultant will find one that is not only close to what you had in mind but also fits you. The smaller the built structure is, the more vital it is to construct it to the exact prescribed size. In other words, even more care must be taken to be accurate in following the *Ayadi* for a piece of jewelry than for a large building.

Everything has its own vibratory quality. *Ayadi* calculations adjust the house or other created object to fit the vibrational wavelength of the individuals for whom it is intended. Now that this knowledge has been revived, it provides the opportunity to truly create home as sanctuary, a sacred space that is tailored to and totally supportive of its inhabitants. *Ayadi* calculations create an environment that connects you to earth and cosmic forces in a way that fits you and allows your life to blossom and prosper. To do this, your Vastu expert will make sure that the *Ayadi* calculations and exact dimensions of the home correspond in a beneficial way to your *Nakshatra*, your "lunar mansion" (interestingly, this indicates a grand home) or birth star. Your exact point in time and space determines this vibratory quality. This has been poetically and evocatively referred to in an unconscious but knowing way (the way of poets) by Gaston Bachelard when he describes images in French poetry: "We have the impression that the stars in heaven come to live on earth, that the houses of men form earthly constellations."[15]

There are twenty-seven *Nakshatras* according to Jyotish. These are constellations or star clusters that are the lunar mansions; aptly, as we just discussed, mansions are prosperous, comfortable dwellings. *Ayadi* calculations can also be done without the *Nakshatra* of the future building's inhabitants, if necessary. In that case, *Nama Nakshatra* is used, aligning the first syllable of the name, street, or area with the corresponding *Nakshatra*.

Now that you have become familiar with the elements of Vastu, including the *Vastu Purusha Mandala*, the five elements, the directions, the importance of beauty, and other components that create a vibrant Vastu structure, in Section Three we will look at a Vastu home from the entrance, through all the rooms, and back out into the garden.

parts of a vastu home

V irtually any place can be or become sacred space. It depends on your intention and treatment of the space. A phenomenally supportive, living organism results when you buy Vastu-appropriate land and build according to Vastu guidelines with a trained Vastu professional. But if you don't have this option, focus on what you can do to rectify and enhance the home you already have.

Section Three describes specific features and rooms of the inside and outside of a Vastu home, which utilize the basics of Vastu described in Section Two, such as the grid pattern of the *Vastu Purusha Mandala*, the importance of the mother wall, the directions and five elements, beauty, the use of color, and Ayadi calculations.

Land: The Foundation of a Vastu Home

If you want to build according to Vastu, the first thing to look at is the land you are considering. The land is the foundation for your building; it has a profound effect on the energy that will be embodied in your home. Consider its color and taste, what it's next to (roads and other buildings), what its shape is, where the trees or any water on the property are. One traditional test involves digging a hole in the land and then refilling it with the same soil. If the soil fills up the hole or overflows, buy the land and build. If the soil does not fill up the hole, consider looking elsewhere for a home site.

Many areas that we build in today might not have been considered optimal for human habitation in Vastu's seminal days. If you love the landscape of your town or state but it is not Vastu-compliant in its qualities, don't worry about it. What is, is. We live in a beautiful but not perfect world.

An auspicious site is ideally square or rectangular in shape. Stella Kramrisch, the renowned India scholar and author of *The Hindu Temple*, speaks of the square as being "literally the fundamental form of Indian architecture" and "the archetype and pattern of order."[1] If you've already moved into a home and the lot is an irregular shape, Vastu recommends that you correct its irregularity with fencing, a compound wall, or a hedge of shrubs that creates a rectangular site on your lot. You can also trim the lot into a rectangle and give or sell the "leftover" bits of land to your neighbor, so that you can have a more supportive shape (and therefore energy) to your building site. Similarly, if there is a bite missing from your rectangle, you can approach the owner of the neighboring lot to negotiate its purchase, which would benefit you both.

Another point regarding your neighbors' homes: Vastu recommends against your living in a small building or plot of land squished in between two much larger neighbors. As you might have figured out from its metaphorical implications, it creates an oppressed atmosphere of continual lack compared to others.

Vastu discourages the purchase of a lot that has trash or inauspicious material on it. There are guidelines that refer specifically to such items as bones, anthills, termites, and other unappealing things. It is of course also preferable that any former occupants of the home or land were happy and successful in life.

If you're not lucky enough to have a natural stream or pond, you can add a water feature in the northeast of the property and get the same freshness and prosperity benefits. For existing water features, the correct water flow direction for a healthy effect is clockwise. The founders of a proposed Ayurveda clinic and school in Wisconsin asked me to evaluate land they were considering buying; fortunately the river flows by their land in a clockwise direction.

Some Vastu guidelines differ depending on if you are building a chapel or a home. According to Vastu, the ideal shape for homes and most buildings is square or rectangular. There are also other, more varied choices to be made in conjunction with a Vastu-trained architect who knows how to add harmonious extensions and additions of various shapes that are mathematically based on the grid pattern of the *Vastu Purusha Mandala*. There are specific rules that your Vastu expert will follow. Your Vastu home will not look just like every other Vastu home; it can have extensions of various sizes and shapes from the mother wall, so long as they are designed by an architect who knows how to modulate those shapes in proportion and correct placement. Curves are entirely acceptable as long as they are properly placed and designed according to the grid pattern of *Vastu Purusha Mandala*. The mother wall itself, however, must be rectangular or square, although again there is one alternate design that can be utilized by a trained Vastu professional.

Shapes have an effect on the flow of energy within the space. Circular or polygonal shapes can be used for community spaces but not for your home or residential plot of land. Circles, triangles, and polygons are considered to be too active in their effect and therefore agitating energetically for human habitation.

Orientation

Proper orientation of the house is critically important in Vastu. As mentioned previously, the house should not be oriented to the intermediate directions of northeast, southeast, southwest, and northwest. Some people have heard that their front entrance should face northeast. This is a misunderstanding. Very nourishing spiritual energy enters from the excellent northeast direction, but it is not an acceptable placement for the front door. In fact, the corners of a building are never good choices for a door.

The sides of the home should be aligned with the cardinal directions of north, south, east, and west. Ideally, the orientation will be a tiny bit off true east in the direction of the northeast in order to have a successful life in the world. There are benefits to each of the four cardinal directions for the orientation of your home. Vastu architect Michael Borden described them to me as follows: "South brings salvation and redemption from earthly worries, a west entrance is for material prosperity and big numbers, north is for wealth, and an east entrance endows the occupants with physical comfort and mental peace."[1] Ganapati Sthapati has also described homes with the front facing east as having the quality of bringing comfort.

Front Door Placement

Proper placement of the front door is paramount in Vastu. Each of the four cardinal directions has two or three auspicious *padas* for door placement. A north-facing home is the only one that can beneficially have a central door, although some central door placements work well for other types of buildings, like medical facilities and temples.

This diagram of the *Vastu Purusha Mandala* illustrates all the *padas* in each of the four directions that are good for a home's front door placement. There are a total of nine *padas* out of thirty-two that, when used for the front door, give an auspicious effect to the home's inhabitants. The other twenty-three predispose the occupants to various negative tendencies. Although Ganapati Sthapati rarely speaks of rectification and instead insists that people build correctly according to Vastu, there are a few stories floating around that tell of his providing rectification. One of these stories involves

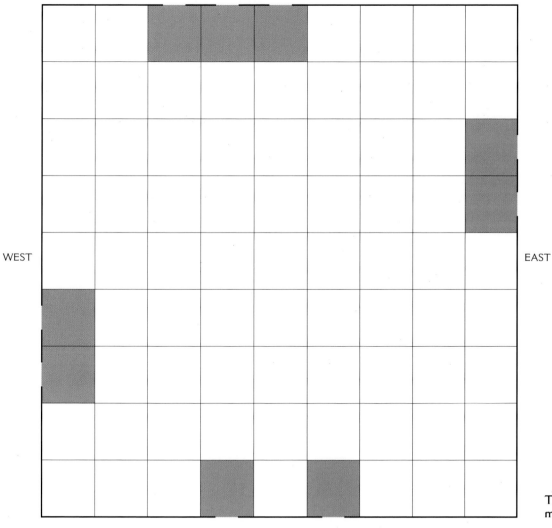

NORTH

WEST

EAST

SOUTH

There are nine options for the proper placement of a home's front door.

front door placement. Apparently there was a young woman in India who very much wanted to be married but had no offers. She approached Sthapati and begged him to help her. He told her to have the front door of her home moved to an auspicious position that would bring benefit—and a husband—into her life. She insisted that she needed help immediately and couldn't wait for the renovations to be done. He had her go home and draw the outline of a correctly placed new front door to her home on the wall with chalk and empower it with her focused intention. It worked. She went to a party that evening and met her future husband.

If you are constructing a home, center the door in the middle of an appropriate *pada* of the grid pattern. This also makes a big difference in the remodeling of an older home. Vastu builder Jessie Mercay's construction workers thought she was crazy to spend time and money moving the front door of an old house to a different position, but they immediately noticed the difference in how the house felt after the door's placement was changed.

One of the best choices for front door placement is the fourth *pada* from the right when you are facing the house (the fourth from the left if you are standing at the front of the house facing outward). Since especially auspicious energies flow toward the house from the east and the north, those five entrance possibilities are excellent choices. This is another demonstration of how an exact adherence to measurements is vital in Vastu. Here is an example of the effect of one particular choice of entrance *pada*. The fourth *pada* entrance on the north is called *Indra pada*. Indra is viewed in the Vedic tradition as the sovereign of heaven; having the front door of your home in *Indra pada* brings the influence of "name and fame," according to Sthapati. This reflects the position of Indra, its *pada devata*, who is the ruler of the heavens.

The front door, wherever it is placed, should be unobstructed; no body of water, tree, or pole should block it or the approach of rays of early morning sunlight. The front door, as befits the main entrance to and metaphorical mouth of your home, should be the largest door of the house.

Threshold and Entryway

A threshold is a sacred thing.

—Greek Philosopher Porphyrus

Vastu recommends keeping your home fresh and clean to welcome the divine. This includes keeping the approach and entrance to your home clean, welcoming, and well maintained. If you like a distressed look, make sure to keep it in good condition. Two clients in Santa Fe had splintering, unpainted wooden gates that were a hazard and an eyesore—certainly not a desirable approach to their homes. Replacing the gates with new, freshly painted ones made a huge difference. One woman mentioned during the consultation that she found it challenging to walk to the front door from her car in the winter—the sidewalk had cracked and sunk, encouraging water and ice to accumulate, which made it dangerous to reach the house. Clearly, these were not good metaphorical messages to be sending herself and the world (not to mention that it was a potential

liability issue). I recommended that she replace the gate and put in a new, level, slightly raised path of paving stones interspersed with an herb ground cover. She planted creeping thyme between the stones and loved the effect; now she has a beautiful, inviting, and safe entrance.

Cobwebs, dirt, peeling paint, and disrepair send out a message of poverty and a lower vibration than you would want for your home's first impression. If there is room without making the entry seem cramped, put pots of healthy plants on each side of your door. If the temperature in your region falls below freezing, ask your local nursery about hardy evergreens that can survive the winter in pots outside your front door. You can supplement these anchor plants with pots of flowers the rest of the year.

A common problem when people are overwhelmed is letting clutter accumulate on the front porch by the door. Avoid having anything here that is not useful or attractive. Unfinished projects drain your energy, and seeing a collection of discarded objects and uncompleted projects gives a burdened, harried impression.

Many people enter their homes through the garage instead of through the front door. If you can, enter the home through the front door instead, so long as it is properly placed. Be sure that the attention paid to the condition and beauty of the front door is also given to the door from the garage into the house. Is it clean and painted? Is it well lighted and welcoming? If the door is scuffed up and dreary, you are sending yourself that message every time you go through it. You will feel more uplifted if you lavish some care on this important entrance. I also recommend choosing an auspicious section of the *Vastu Purusha Mandala* grid, as discussed above, for placement of the door between the house and garage if you use it instead of the front door.

Traditionally in India, doors are not left unadorned. If you do not have an elaborately carved front door, you can add something meaningful: an image of Ganesha, the remover of obstacles and protector of women; emblems of peace and expansiveness such as the Om (also transliterated as "Aum") symbol; an image of Lakshmi, the goddess of wealth and prosperity; or anything else you find potent and meaningful as a blessing for the home.

You can enhance your entrance door without making changes that will cause trouble with your homeowners' association. For instance, I decorated the front door of a condominium using rubber stamps of Ganesha and a lotus flower, which I stamped seven times each on the door with a gold ink pad. The effect is subtle but beautiful. Hanging seasonal live wreaths also adds a rich, welcoming flourish to your front door. Elements of beauty always rev up the energy and are integral components of Vastu.

There are wonderful folk traditions in India in which women decorate the exterior walls of their homes, frequently with raised designs. I saw a demonstration of this at the Craft Museum in New Delhi. Wouldn't more people feel connected to their homes if they literally got their hands into it, like this woman?

You can also adopt the ancient custom of creating what are called *kolam*, *mandana*, *alpona*, or *rangoli*, depending on the region of India, at the threshold of your home. These are made with rice flour, colored powder, or with white coloring dribbled from a wet rag.

I photographed this striking piece of personal process art in Bangalore, India, during a walk in a residential neighborhood. It is a *kolam*, ritual rice powder offering created at dawn at the home's threshold.

Women traditionally create these spiritual artworks each morning to bless the home and to invoke Lakshmi's loving attention. These are usually abstract images but may also depict plant forms, deities, humans, or animals. This folk art form is related to *mandalas* and *yantras*. It is ephemeral artwork, one in which process is more important than product. A new one will be created the next day to replace the old one worn away by footprints and the industrious harvesting of the rice powder by nature's tiny hungry creatures. These drawings are made with colored powders or with flowers in some regions of India, so you have a choice of media for your own artistic offerings. Many Indian women keep sketchbooks with ideas for *kolams*, and there are competitions in India for the best ones. Everyone, regardless of their religion—Hindu, Christian, Jain—participates in these community competitions. Photographer and ethnologist Stephen Huyler writes, "It is the only art in India that transcends caste, occupation, and religion."[2] The making of *kolams* is a spiritual technique that can transform the experience of the artist. Writer-dancer Chandralekha, who once spent days creating *kolams*, described it by saying "Everything around me became points, dancing points in space, stretching out towards infinity."[3]

Vamsa Danda: Your Home's Spine of Light

Vastu recommends that your home have a clear, straight path through it from the front door to a back door or window. This allows the continual passage of light, air, and solar energy for nourishment of the house. The *vamsa danda* ("spine of light," "bamboo pole," or "backbone") or *brahma danda* ("spine or thread of spirit") enhances the flow of *prana* to radiate throughout your entire dwelling. It is a pleasant feature in its effect, both visually and energetically, for houses with a *vamsa danda* do not feel as closed in and stagnant as homes without one. Feng Shui thinks that this feature allows *ch'i* to move so quickly through the space that you miss out on its benefits. This Feng Shui belief is not based on scientific principles. Vastu explains that this feature is very positive and enhances the circulation of air and energy throughout the home. If you're used to working with Feng Shui, be open to looking from this newly presented perspective, for it will pay off.

If you find that there is a long, vacant, uninterrupted space in the building that goes from one end to the other, then of course add some beautiful furnishings for energetic and aesthetic purposes. Having a *vamsa danda* has no negative effects, only positive ones.

In temples, the *vamsa danda* runs straight through the center of the building. For homes and other structures, the *vamsa danda's* placement depends on the location of the entrance door and back door. As previously discussed, it is best to have the front door in one of the segments of the grid pattern of the *Vastu Purusha Mandala* that is known to be vibrationally positive for an entrance.

If your *vamsa danda* is blocked and there is no door or window opposite it, Sthapati suggested to me drilling a tiny hole in the wall opposite the front door so that there can be a breath running through it. This is not a practical solution for most Americans, but the suggestion itself shows the importance of the *vamsa danda* and perhaps will serve as an incentive to install a window or door opposite the front door to improve the feeling and energy of the home. People who already have a *vamsa danda* in their home have experienced its benefit in another way as well. If you have ever walked in the front door of a house with this Vastu feature, you know that you still feel connected to nature: you can see through the back window or door to the beauty of the landscape behind the home. You know from this experience how valuable and delightful the *vamsa danda* is. The *vamsa danda* helps the house and its occupants maintain connection and feel more in tune with nature.

Vastu builder Jessie Mercay remodeled a neglected house using Vastu guidelines. When she wanted to show me what she had done to rectify the house, I was hesitant to walk inside, since the exterior was still run-down and unpleasant. To my surprise, it felt good, due to her moving the front door to an auspicious *pada* and creating a *vamsa danda*. I was comfortable and enjoyed being there, even though it was still in rough shape.

In another instance, a Boulder, Colorado, chiropractor, who believes in Vastu because of his experience with the effect of changes we made to his home, got a Feng Shui consultation on his new office space. The Feng Shui consultant unwittingly created unease in his mind by pointing out that there was a straight pathway from the entry door that penetrated the office space to the windows on the back wall, and she wanted to block this flow with solid doors. After hearing about the benefits of the *vamsa danda*, the chiropractor understood the metaphor, realized that he could sense the energetic benefits of the *vamsa danda*, and saw that the feature was perfect for a space that focused on the healing of human spines. This relieved his mind, and he kept the beneficial *vamsa danda* open.

My clients report great benefit from the subtle spiritual science of Vastu and its application to their homes. Another Boulder client wrote me after moving into and living in her new home that has a clear *vamsa danda* and a well-placed east-facing front door: "I feel like an entirely new person in my new home." A Chicago client stated that everything improved for his family when they moved into a home with a clear *vamsa danda* and a correctly positioned north entrance.

Brahmasthan: The Nourishing Center of Your Home

The *Brahmasthan*, the center of each room and the center of the building, is one of the most vital features of Vastu, since it is the area from which energy is self-generated into the home from within the structure of the *Vastu Purusha Mandala*. The space element, *akasha*, is predominant here. The central 3 x 3 *padas* of the *Vastu Purusha Mandala*'s 9 x 9 grid pattern should be left open with no walls, beams, heavy weights, or blockages. At the very least, keep the single centermost *pada* of the *Brahmasthan* open. When building, keep fireplaces, toilets, walls, utilities, etc., out of this central section of the *Vastu Purusha Mandala* grid. The center of each room should also be treated in this way: avoid putting heavy pieces of furniture here. Vastu recommends placing a skylight or cupola with clerestory windows above the *Brahmasthan*. Ideally the skylight is the same size as the centermost *pada*. Ordering a custom skylight is a worthwhile investment for your home that will bring great energetic benefit.

If you do not have a clearly defined, open *Brahmasthan* and cannot make structural changes, there are a few small techniques you can use to honor the *Brahmasthan* and recognize its energies. I have used luminous gold paint to decorate and define the central grid *pada* on the ceiling to at least acknowledge its importance. This is a minor way to recognize the *Brahmasthan*, but it was all that I could do in that home besides installing *yantras*, since the walls could not be moved. Installing the Vedic Pyramid, which combines *mantras*, *yantras*, and pyramids, will alleviate some of the negative influence of a blocked *Brahmasthan* on an energetic level. However, nothing other than an open Brahmasthan will give your home the true effect of proper Vastu design.

Opposite: This home benefits from both a *vamsa danda* and clockwise stairs. These features increase beneficial solar and earth energies and *prana* in the house.

Opposite: The *Brahmasthan* of this Santa Fe home has a skylight over it, which connects the center of the house with cosmic energies.

Left: You can decorate the *Brahmasthan* with a rug or a floor inlay, such as this beautiful example from contemporary Indian architect Charles Correa, who appreciates both contemporary design and the value of concepts from India's heritage.

Next page: This home in India, also designed by Charles Correa, has an open courtyard for a *Brahmasthan*, which cools the home and connects it with the sky.

The *Brahmasthan* is the lung and the heart of the house. If you wish to create a home for your heart, honor the architectural structure's heart. Women's emotions in particular can be affected by an obstructed *Brahmasthan*.

The *Brahmasthan* of the house can be a central courtyard open to the sky. This is a wonderful feature to enjoy a close connection with nature.

Staircases

Stairs should move in a clockwise direction from the ground up, in order to align with the natural clockwise movement of beneficial earth energies. This knowledge is found in many world cultures. For example, Native American traditions recognize the use of the clockwise spiral to bring in beneficial earth energy. Risers should be an odd number, not an even number.

Staircases should be in the southwest or south or in extensions from the mother wall. If the climate permits, stairs are ideal on the outside of the house; you can also place the stairs in a covered extension from the mother wall. Avoid placing stairs and other heavy structures in the corners of the grid pattern. Staircases should not be in the *Brahmasthan*, the very center of the house; they are too heavy for an area that should be kept clear and open. If the stairs are already there and can't be moved, keep them spotless and clear and use rectification tools from Vedic sacred geometry's *yantras*, such as the Vedic Pyramid, to help alleviate some of the strain on spatial energies.

Balconies, Patios, and Portals

Balconies, porches, patios, loggias, portals, and verandas, whether they are transitional zones or completely outdoor areas, are ideally on the east or north sides of your building. This enables the nourishing energies from those directions to easily enter and fill the space. In sunbelt regions, covered portals on the south and west sides help protect the interior of the house from overheating and too much direct ultraviolet penetration. These transitional areas should be considered living space that is decorated in a thoughtful, relaxed manner. Do not leave them vacant or littered with trash or items left from the previous season, which gives the area an abandoned look. Potted plants, comfortable seating, and the use of natural materials in your décor here as elsewhere in your home enhances the interface between the inside and outside of the building, between the built structure and nature.

This covered patio at Sunrise Springs in Santa Fe provides a lovely spot in nature to relax.

In temperate climates, an open loggia facing the courtyard is a sensible and beautiful way to add extra living space and connection with nature. You may want to add bamboo blinds that you can roll down to protect the area during inclement weather.

Rooms

This section explains the rooms of a Vastu transcendental home. Color recommendations for individual rooms are not given here, since use of color frequently depends on directional placement of the room rather than the type of room itself, and existing homes are not usually in accord with Vastu guidelines for directional placement. To choose color schemes, refer back to Section Two.

bedroom

The master bedroom is ideally in the southwest, the calm, grounded territory of the earth element. Avoid sleeping in the southeast, since the fire element is strong there and can disrupt sleep, weaken your health, and inflame emotions. If your bedroom is in the southeast and you absolutely cannot move it, you can move the bed's placement into the southwest quadrant of the room to harness its more solid, earthy nature and install a Venus yantra face up underneath the mattress. If you have a lot of *vata* in your constitution, sleeping in the northwest, which is governed by the air element, may be too agitating; but northwest could be a good choice for people who have *kapha* constitutions, since the subtle energy could help enliven their tendency to be a bit sluggish. Usually northwest is recommended for the guest room, since you want guests to come for an enjoyable but brief visit and then move on again. Movement is of course a quality of the air element.

Keep the television out of the bedroom. Its electrical radiation and stimulating subject matter are not conducive to a restful space. Keep the bedroom a serene, beautiful, and private space; it should be a peaceful retreat for sleep and intimacy, a sanctuary. Make the bedroom a work-free zone so that your mind and the room can settle down to a less busy energy. If there is no other place in the entire home for your workstation and computer, find a beautiful screen to partition it off, or cover it with a sumptuous piece of fabric when not in use. This will symbolically honor the needed separation of activities, help settle down the active energy of working, and allow better sleep.

Although they are beautiful, positive features, some spiritual objects and altars can generate too much energy in the bedroom and disrupt your ability to sleep. Place these in another room. Including a favorite picture or statue of this nature in your bedroom is just fine; artwork in general is an excellent idea for the bedroom. Position something you find truly lovely across from your bed so that you see it when you first open your eyes in the morning. This can be a tapestry, painting, photograph, or a window with a view of nature. Keep pictures of your parents, children, and relatives in another room; however, happy pictures of yourself and your partner or of ideal, divine couples like Radha and Krishna or Shiva and Parvati create a good effect in the bedroom.

It's best not to position the bedroom over a garage. Exhaust and oil leaks on the garage floor can enter the bedroom from a garage below it, and the rising fumes can make you sick. I advised clients whose bedroom was above the garage to have their unfinished garage ceiling sealed, the clutter removed, and the garage floor cleaned. They reported that their sleep improved after they

implemented these suggestions. Since wise Vastu guidelines call for detached garages, this is not an issue that comes up in a home designed according to Vastu.

Vastu advises against metal beds since metal brings in a complication of electromagnetic fields that can affect your health and your ability to sleep. Use a wooden bed frame and headboard, or one that is constructed of other all natural materials: wood, bamboo, silk, wool, etc. Headboards are a desirable plus; they give metaphorical and literal support. Footboards can create a feeling of being restricted and trapped inside a limiting box. Don't be hemmed in with your head and feet too close to a solid surface.

Sleep with your head in the east or south, which is healing. Do not have your head and pillow in the north, since this is draining, aging, and does not allow as deep a rest. The human body has magnetic polar energies; if your head is in the northern polar direction, it produces a negative effect. Studies have been done by proponents of one version of Vastu, Maharishi Sthapatya Veda, that indicate that people who sleep with their heads in the north are much more likely to be anxious and depressed than those who sleep with their heads in the south or east. West is considered somewhat neutral for head placement for sleeping. If your head is pointed between two cardinal directions, you will receive the effect of both directions. If at all possible, arrange your bed so that your head will lie in the east to south range. Overhead beams are a popular structural decoration but not a healthy one to sleep beneath, since they create dissonant energy. Add a canopy or use push pins to drape fabric above the bed to protect you from the oppressive energy of beams above your body.

Vastu recommends that all spaces be clean and orderly. If you have trouble sleeping, a bed that has been prepared with fresh sheets provides a welcoming sense of well-being and relaxation to send you off to sleep.

children's room

Children's bedrooms are not that different from adult bedrooms. Children and adults alike need private space that is well organized, personal, and has a good flow. On the other hand, children usually find it easier to fall asleep and stay asleep than their parents do, so it is okay to keep toys, desks, and projects in the bedroom. The young son and daughter of Newport, Rhode Island, clients loved the changes in their bedrooms that were made after our initial consultation. All we did was rearrange a few pieces of furniture. The main suggestion was to move the head of the beds, which had originally been poorly placed in the north.

The main point to remember when designing children's rooms is to listen closely to the children: What are their interests? What colors and decorations make them light up and express their personal style? Do not simply impose your own preferences upon them without finding what truly fits their individuality and desires, whether they openly express them or not. As long as it does not conflict with Vastu guidelines and thus create more problems in the home, listen to and attend to your children's needs as you would an adult.

This inviting bedroom benefits from natural fibers. All of its soft, luxurious bedding is silk.

bathroom

Bathrooms should look and feel light, clean, and fresh. Ideally, there will be a window that opens. If there isn't, you can add a plug-in air purifier, good lighting, and plants. Many people find it useful to keep incense and matches or essential oils and a diffuser on the bathroom counter.

Although there is evidence of indoor plumbing in Mohenjo-Daro, which follows many Vastu guidelines, toilets were supposedly not inside the house when Vastu was formulated. Keeping the toilet lid down is a Feng Shui recommendation that is compatible with Vastu and improves energy. Since indoor bathrooms were not assigned specific locations in the Vastu tradition, extensions from the mother wall are perfect placements for them. In addition to what is described here, there are many specific guidelines for bathroom placement that trained Vastu experts will use for your new home. If you are building a new home, a Vastu consultant is necessary; a full explanation of all factors and guidelines is beyond the scope of this book.

There are a variety of suggestions for contemporary bathroom placement besides in extensions from the mother wall. They can be in the northwest or west. Some suggest that a good place for the bathroom is on the east side of the house because of the early morning's ultraviolet rays, which are purifying. I noticed this in the home of a New Jersey couple whose eastern bathroom has a large central skylight over the room's *Brahmasthan* and both a window and a door to the garden on the eastern wall. This fresh-feeling bathroom also benefits from large, healthy houseplants that are like sculptural works of art and from a large mirror set off with a silver-painted wooden frame.

Bathrooms should never be in the northeast or in the center of the house. Their placement in these areas is considered to be particularly inauspicious, since it puts impure substances in energetically vital spots. If you have more than one bathroom, consider removing any bathrooms in the northeast or *Brahmasthan*. If your only bathroom is in one of these areas and you cannot move it, keep it scrupulously clean, light, and fresh. If the bathroom is located in the northeast, include a water feature such as a fountain to honor the water element. Another potent improvement for northeast bathrooms is the use of *Ketu* and Jupiter *yantras*, specific appeasements or honoring recognitions of the planetary rulers of northeastern energies, which are described in Section Four of this book. You can also place a *Vastu Purusha Yantra* on the wall of a bathroom that is badly located; use a wall across from the mirror so that the yantra and its energetic effect is doubled. I have placed all three of these *yantras* in a northeast bathroom and felt the energy lighten and expand.

If your bathroom is in the southeast, which is not appropriate since southeast is the realm of *agni*, the fire element, at least honor the element through the use of color. I had this situation in my Boulder condo and found the room felt a lot better when I brought in beautiful red towels. So did a Santa Fe client who applied this and my other suggestions to his southeast bathroom and then raved that "amazingly, even my once-funky bathroom now has a shrine-like serenity." If there is a soap dish that collects water in the shower stall in a southeast bathroom, as I had in this home, be mindful that it is not the right placement of this element and make sure to empty the water out of the dish. You can also add candles to honor the fire element. Since it is not safe to leave candles unattended, another technique I used was to leave the light on in the bathroom from the time I got up in the morning until I went to sleep at night. In addition to acknowledging *agni*, it provided sufficient light in a windowless bathroom to keep houseplants quite happy. The extra energy usage was more than compensated for by the additional beauty, *prana,* and oxygen provided by the plants. At night, a little night light honors that fire element in a southeast area.

kitchen

Kitchens belong in the southeast, the direction where the fire element of *agni* is predominant. *Agni*'s color is infrared. Subtle infrared rays are most prevalent in this direction and considered beneficial, especially for women.

Don't use microwave ovens, which destroy the *prana* or life-force in food and render it into something dead that does not nourish. Microwave ovens dissolve the harmonically beneficial influence of nature in food. If you want speedy cooking and healthy food, use a convection oven. Professional cooks love these ovens since they cook evenly and are less drying.

You may want to follow the lovely custom of having a northeast kitchen altar to express gratitude for all your household's nourishing blessings of food. Keep the area clean and beautiful and devise a simple personal ritual for giving thanks for abundant food. If you like, you can include candles, incense, water, and a picture or statue of a favorite deity or saint. San Pasqual is the patron saint of cooking and is honored in Hispanic Catholic areas. Abundance of grains and other foods is one of the eight aspects of Lakshmi, the goddess of abundance in the Vedic tradition. By honoring these blessings, the kitchen is bountiful and nourishes the household.

Sometimes kitchen décor can be dictated by structural deficiencies. For example, if there are no windows in your kitchen, there are tricks you can use to brighten it up and create views and a more expansive, less closed-in feeling. I used a mirror framed by a colorfully painted Haitian iron sculpture of birds, trees, and flowers at the end of one kitchen. In another home with a wall instead of a window above the kitchen sink, I placed a framed picture of Lakshmi on that wall so the homeowners would have something beautiful and inspirational to look at while doing the not always uplifting chore of dishwashing. The glass of its frame reflected sky, trees, and mountains that were otherwise only seen from the living room. In addition, the sun was rising behind Lakshmi in this poster, so it enhanced the solar energy that should have been entering through a window on this eastern wall if it had not been blocked by a neighboring condo in the building.

Vastu does not really include the use of mirrors, but certain placements of mirrors can enhance the energy of your home without conflicting with Vastu rules. A universally applicable, beneficial placement of a mirror is on the wall behind the stove. This opens up the room, adds light, and makes it easy to relax, since you can see what is going on behind you.

Kitchens can be arranged according to the five elements if you are designing your home and can plan the layout in advance. The heaviest items, including the refrigerator and storage, go in the

Above: A professional cook avoided the dilemma of blocking the center of the *Brahmasthan* by splitting the work island in the middle of her kitchen. This opened it up as a passageway that also allows her to easily pass between the stove and refrigerator.

south, west, or southwest. If you can face east while cooking and preparing food, that will bring the most peaceful, energizing influence into the food. It also benefits the cook. The stove belongs in the southeast sector, which is the fire element. The sink goes in the north or northeast, where the water element predominates. Leave some room in the northeast corner for a kitchen shrine. The dishwasher, since it involves both electricity (fire) and water, could go anywhere along the east side of the room, where the energy of water and fire reside. Many kitchens have center islands, but this conflicts with Vastu. Leave the center of the room open to honor the *Brahmasthan*.

Right: The placement of the stove in this southeast kitchen allows the cook to face east, which is the most beneficial configuration for a kitchen. The room's central *Brahmasthan* is unobstructed and has a central skylight overhead.

Opposite: This personal kitchen altar next to an immaculate sink graces the northeast of another Santa Fe home.

Your laundry facilities may be next to the kitchen or in a separate area. This area, like the dishwasher, involves both fire and water elements. Ideally you will have doors to partition it off and create a quieter atmosphere. Your washer and dryer will benefit from an occasional cleaning, and the vibration of the space will go up.

dining room

Some sources recommend that the dining room be on the west side of the house; others recommend the east side. Clearly the room should be close to the kitchen for convenience and practicality. Some say that the dining room table must be rectangular or square, and that a round table makes people eat too fast because it is a shape with active movement, but I have seen no evidence for this. I have never noticed any ill effect from having a round table for dining, and I enjoy eating and lingering at the table! This guideline about shape is not intended for furniture but for the shape of the house.

Enjoy your meals in a serene, attractive setting with artwork that you like, unchipped dishes, and flatware that fits your hand. The whole experience should be aesthetically pleasing. Food is more nourishing when you sit comfortably, eat with awareness, and take time to enjoy the flavor instead of eating on the run. There is an expression in India, "Food is *Brahman*," which means that food is the divine wholeness bestowed upon you. Eating with awareness allows you to honor the gift of the food, which is often taken for granted. Food is one of the main sources from which we obtain *prana*. Eating with awareness allows you to absorb more of the *prana* from the food. So drop the hectic, busy pace of life, at least while you are eating. Take an attitude of mindfulness and consider the food as *prasad*, a gift from the divine intended to nurture your inner and outer development and your ability to flourish in life.

Many people only use their "good" silver and dishes for special occasions a few times a year. Why not experience inspiration on all occasions? Bring celebration and honoring to every day you can; this acknowledges the specialness of every moment and expresses gratitude for it. If you have real silverware, use it on a daily basis. Silver has a healthier effect on the body than steel, which is part of the reason that people enjoy it.

Although Vastu recommends keeping the *Brahmasthan* of all rooms open, practicality must prevail in the placement of the dining room table, so keeping the room's center clear is not something to worry about.

living room

When the living room is used for festive gatherings, musical events, spiritual meetings, and ceremonies, it can be well placed in the *Brahmasthan* of the home. Beloved musical instruments such as pianos bring a greater feeling of relationship into the living room by bringing family and friends together in the space.

In this plate of food

I see the entire universe

supporting my existence.

—THICH NHAT HANH

This uplifting laundry room is well placed in the northwest and benefits from a window that opens.

Vastu living rooms and family rooms are usually in the north or west. A comfortable, welcoming living room is useful and enjoyable in both homes and business spaces. Furnish it with some upholstered pieces and anything else that you feel is appropriate, but take care not to add so much furniture that it overwhelms the space and makes it hard to navigate between seating and tables. For optimal arrangement of furniture, face east or north when sitting and place the heavy pieces in the west and south. If you enjoy reading in this room, include a good reading lamp next to your chair. Place tables in useful spots. Choose natural materials, as discussed in Section Two, whenever possible. Fireplaces and electrical equipment such as the TV, DVD player, and stereo are best in the southeast of the room, where the fire element is predominant.

home work spaces

Study/Office. Studies can be placed in the northeast of the home. The study area for children is usually in the west. Everyone should face east or north for the best brainwave activity when studying. Sometimes having your desk face a window can create eyestrain and headaches, especially if you are facing south, due to too much glare. If possible, do not have your back flush against windows. Facing directly into a wall can restrict your creativity; a better choice is to face into the room, which creates a more expansive feeling.

Don't skimp on the size of the desk. Having too little desktop space can make you feel overwhelmed. You need space for your computer system and for writing by hand. Only keep those books, supplies, entertainment, and papers in your study that truly fit and are conducive to the room's purpose, and keep them organized. Lighting should be glare-free and adequate for working without eyestrain.

The skeptical husband of one of my clients, who got angry every time she brought up her desire to use Vastu in their home, completely shifted his view after we made some changes in their study. He really experienced how the use of basic Vastu principles opened up the space, and now he loves the feel of the room. He told her, "I've really got to hand it to you. Vastu works! I didn't want to go in the study before, and now it is my favorite room in the house." All we did was move existing furniture into a different configuration and relocate one bookshelf to the hallway. Originally, a tall, heavy filing cabinet was in the northeast corner of the room, which was poorly placed and felt oppressive, since the northeast should be kept more light and open. An armchair located in the northwest did not allow the owners to feel at ease for very long, since the quality of movement is strong in that sector of any architectural space. As the clients said, the room was uninviting. We moved the filing cabinet from the northeast to the northwest of the room and immediately felt the difference. The armchair, which is much lighter and lower than the filing cabinet, ended up in the northeast. The computer remained in the southeast, which is good placement for anything electrical. The client reported, "Now you feel all the lightness from the northeast and you want to

I always think of the place

I work as holy.

—ALICE WALKER

enter the room." Her husband also loved our choice of a golden-yellow color for the walls of this northeast room, which is rich and striking with the homeowners' dark wood Mission-style furniture. The color is appropriate for the planet Jupiter, the directional lord of the northeast location of the room, and provides a feeling of warmth to the room, especially in the winter months when it is most needed.

This "conversion" story was a dramatic moment: someone who didn't believe in Vastu actually experienced the difference in the room and acknowledged it. Vastu is an experience. Architecture

This art studio and office has an open Brahmasthan,
which gives a more expansive feeling to this very active
room. The desk and painting table are placed so that the
artist and writer faces north and east when working.

is an experience. Because of that experience, my client can now openly talk about Vastu with the architects who are designing the addition to their home.

Studio. Many people have art or design studios or woodworking shops in their homes. This section was a natural one for me to include in this book, since I am an artist and personally consider a studio to be one of the most important rooms in a home with some of the most specific requirements. The northwest of your studio is a good place to keep your inventory or goods for sale, since movement characterizes the northwest sector. Since the air element is predominant in the northwest, this is also the best placement for wind chimes, wind streamers, and prayer flags. Be sure to have opening windows in this area, and use them to bring fresh air into your space.

Since the southeast is the area of the fire element, this is the area to place a kiln, if you are a ceramicist. All artists know to have good ventilation to the outside of the building when they are using materials that can present a health hazard. Windows that open and an exhaust fan are practical necessities for most art studios.

All things electrical will ideally be located in the southeast quadrant of your studio. Your sound system can be placed here on built-in shelving, and you can place your computer, scanner, and printer here as well.

If you paint on paper, canvas, or fabric on the wall, attach the material to the north or east wall. If you work flat on a table or with an easel, face north or east to paint. This will enable you to face a direction that enhances mental clarity and creativity.

Keep the northeast corner and quadrant as clear and open as you can. This is an ideal location for an altar or shrine to honor and acknowledge your creativity and its source. You may wish to include an image of Saraswati, the goddess of the arts, in this area, or her Japanese counterpart, Benten or Benzei-ten.

The southwest is the best place for heavy items and anything related to the earth element. If you have room for plants in your studio, place some in the southwest. Plants can also go in the north to boost your career and finances.

Studios quickly become full of art materials, finished works, and ongoing projects. The room will feel more open and expansive if you remember to honor the *Brahmasthan* of the room by keeping the center area clean, clear, and open.

When you have the opportunity to design your own studio, place the entrance in an auspicious *pada* of the *Vastu Purusha Mandala*, as discussed in Section Two, if the studio is a freestanding building. Place windows in the north or east, if possible, and a window that opens in the northwest. Balconies should be on the north and east sides, not on the south or west, for the best energetic effect.

meditation room

If you are fortunate enough to have an extra room that you can set aside for your meditation, prayers, yoga practice, and contemplative time, it will bring additional spiritual energy and serenity to your home. Some people love the meditative ritual of the Japanese tea ceremony and create a space in their home for this beautiful practice. If you are building, a space for meditation or prayer is an excellent feature to add to the plans. Ideal locations are the northeast or the center of your home. If you are doing *pranayama* or other breathing practices in this space, be sure to include a window that can be opened to allow fresh *prana* into the room.

If you can't devote an entire room for this purpose, you can set up an altar or personal shrine in the northeast of most rooms. Altars for specific purposes can also be erected in their own relevant sector: for example, southwest for relationships, north for finance and career, and northwest for

Right: This meditation room feels grounded and serene from the effect of its natural materials, wood, stone, and adobe.

Opposite: A Japanese tea ceremony room at Sunrise Springs, Santa Fe.

travel or anything represented by movement, which is a characteristic of the air element. Creating an altar honors the divine.

Gardens

Trees and other plants exhale oxygen, providing us with life-sustaining breath. This is one of the reasons they literally enliven any place they are found, whether in the landscape or in buildings. They also purify the air, provide shade, offer raw materials for a multitude of uses, and soothe our eyes and souls with healing green and great beauty. We've all seen two homes next to each other, only one of which has trees and a garden. The lush yard is full of vitality and energy; it uplifts and attracts us. The yard without landscaping is bleak and depressing, which creates the impression that the home is not as prosperous or desirable.

Many of the same basic Vastu guidelines apply to the yard and garden as to the inside of your home or office: Place heavier weight, like rock gardens and stone sculptures, in the south and west instead of in the north and east, which should be kept more open. The southwest is also a good place for a greenhouse, storage area, or potting shed. The south and west are the best places for tall trees to protect and shade the house from the harsh rays that come from these directions. When using metals, such as gardening tools, the best effect comes from copper rather than aluminum or steel. Copper implements heal the soil instead of drying it out or depleting it. Copper rain chains also make a practical and attractive addition to outdoor spaces.

Vastu gardens honor nature and work with it by using organic methods. You may also wish to investigate biodynamic gardening. If your plants are troubled with disease or insects, use *neem* oil spray, friendly insect helpers such as ladybugs and praying mantises, intelligent companion planting, insect-repellant plants like marigolds, and the like before you start using chemicals. Organic gardening books and nurseries can tell you how to combat plant pests and diseases safely and harmoniously. Pesticides and synthetic materials will lower the vibratory energy of your garden. You want an abundance of life energy rather than a lack of *prana* in your garden and home, so be sure to enhance the health of your soil in a natural way.

The best energetic effect and beauty come from the use of natural materials like stone, wood, and bamboo. It will be worth the upkeep. Wood decking is preferable to plastic, and there are non-toxic stains and sealants that you can use instead of toxic conventional applications that can make you ill. Flagstone or other stonework or a brick patio (made with outdoor brick, not indoor brick) are better choices energetically than concrete, which blocks some of the positive earth energies and therefore creates a more sterile effect.

Opposite: A lush, inviting garden created by Marpa Design Studios.

Outdoor water features create a beautiful, soothing, and prosperous influence. Water represents the flow of abundance. The many fountains in Washington, D.C., have made the capital city strong

and wealthy. Water lotuses are an excellent addition, both for their beauty and for their symbolic meaning. Remember that the meaning of symbolism frequently manifests in our world as actual experience. In traditional images, you never see Lakshmi, the goddess of wealth and good fortune, without lotuses. Their completely opened flowers represent abundance and spiritual perfection, so allow lotuses to help bring these features into your life more fully. Choose varieties that work in your climate. You may need to remove them from the garden over the winter months, according to instructions from your water garden nursery.

Streams and rivers should flow clockwise in relation to your property. Do not place ponds, fountains, and waterfalls anywhere other than northeast or north, since water features in any other area will create a negative effect. If they are already there, move them to the northeast or north. Healing medicinal herbs are also well placed in the north or northeast. Remember that the northeast is a sacred zone that should be kept clean, orderly, and pure. In your yard, the northeast is not the place for trash, gardening sheds, or septic systems.

Find joy

in the sky,

in trees,

in flowers.

—Henri Matisse

The northwest is the area for swings, wind streamers, wind chimes, and mobiles, or any other feature that plays with the movement of the wind. Plants that sway in the wind are also well placed in the northwest. This area should not be stagnant; the air should be able to move.

Outdoor kitchens, grills, and fireplaces belong in the southeast, where the fire element rules. If they are currently located in a different direction, move them to prevent distortion of energies. You can add candles here when you have a gathering. Flowers and plants with fiery colors, suggesting red and golden flames, fit well in the southeast of your garden.

You can use the colors associated with the directions and the planets for your garden's color scheme, if you wish. Don't think you have to include all of these colors and items in your garden. It must still have good flow, beauty, and coherence.

The entirety of your lot can be level, or else the south and west should be higher and the north and east lower. Both options are positive according to Vastu guidelines.

Remember the importance of beauty in Vastu and place plants, trees, garden décor, and sculpture that are aesthetically pleasing in the appropriate sectors. An artistically placed urn, lantern, or architectural element can add interest to your garden. You can also use yantras to energize the land, as described in Section Four. Garden ornaments in general should be whatever style you personally are drawn to. Vastu is a universal system; you do not need to make your garden look like India. Any style can be more supportive if the design follows Vastu guidelines.

Certain plants are considered most auspicious for a Vastu garden. Most of the plants mentioned in the traditional Vastu texts are, of course, tropicals that grow in India, but some can be grown almost anywhere. Others can be grown in pots seasonally. Vastu characterizes certain plants as inauspicious or having an undesirable effect. Anyone who has ever bumped into a cactus understands why thorny plants in general are not appropriate for a Vastu-correct garden. Plants with milky sap are also ill-advised. Likewise, some trees have very invasive roots, which can damage the foundations of a home; Vastu recommends against planting such trees. Fruit-bearing trees have the best effect on the household when they are situated in the north or east of your lot. Go for beauty and listen to your intuition when making choices. In general, flowering and medicinal plants are good garden elements. As might be expected, sweetly fragrant plants and flowers are beneficial. Anyone who has ever experienced the bliss of a flower's divine fragrance understands the value of this guideline.

Other garden design tips from Vastu: Plant a grape arbor for abundance. Once you have seen an arbor dripping with grapes, you can grasp its symbolism of overflowing fruitfulness. Pomegranates also generate a good influence.

Other guidelines for yards and gardens include environmentally conscious recommendations of planting trees and setting up a gray water system to help during droughts and water shortages, thus both honoring and listening to the environment. Sri Sri Ravi Shankar has said that if trees are grown, they tend to "draw the clouds." I have noticed that the sections of Santa Fe that have the fewest trees have the least rain and snow and are hotter and less comfortable in the

Gardens bring us to the present moment and open our hearts.

—Martin Mosko, Landscape Architect

Nature is sacred. If you have to cut a tree, you have to ask its permission and promise to plant five more trees. Respect nature. Nature responds to you if you respect it.

—Sri Sri Ravi Shankar

Healing Plants

Some plants radiate even more of a healing influence into the environment than do other plants. Sri Sri Ravi Shankar recommends planting tulsi (holy basil, *Ocimum sanctum*), neem, ashoka (*Saraka indica* or *Jonesia asoka*), and bel (wood apple or Bengal quince, *Aegle marmelos*) to balance and clean the atmosphere. These all grow easily in hot, humid climates like India. If your home's yard doesn't have that ecosystem, you can still grow herbs like tulsi and neem in pots and bring them indoors into a very sunny place in the winter.

Holy basil is tulsi, which means "matchless," and is considered sacred; it boosts the immune system. The consumption of a few tulsi leaves each day prevents illness. *The Yoga of Herbs: An Ayurvedic Guide to Herbal Medicine says*, "[Tulsi] gives the protection of the divine by clearing the aura . . . [It] absorbs positive ions, energizes negative ions, and liberates ozone from the sun's rays." Plant tulsi by the entrance to your home, as is commonly done in India, where paintings of tulsi often frame the front door as well. Om Organics, a company that sells organic tulsi teas, says on its Web site that "according to ancient Indian legends, the plant came into being as an incarnation of the Hindu goddess Tulsi, and is the favoured herb of the gods Vishnu, Ram and Krishna, as well as being revered by Brahma and Shiva. Tulsi is thought to open the heart and mind, and bestow love, compassion, faith and devotion." Seeds of Change, a certified organic seed company, offers organic holy basil (tulsi) seed packets for sale.

Oil preparations from leaves of the neem tree are used as a non-toxic insecticide for gardens as well as in treatments to kill fungus infections. Sometimes you can find neem and tulsi at nurseries and farmer's markets.

The ashoka tree is a flowering evergreen sacred to Kama, the god of love, and to Shiva. According to tradition, it is a deeply healing and protective tree that averts calamities. In Sanskrit, "shoka" means "grief" or "suffering"; since an "a" before a word negates it, "ashoka" means "without grief or suffering." Vaidya R. K. Mishra prescribes ashoka for patients suffering from emotional scars, saying that even the scent of the tree on the breeze is healing. It can be added to an herbal tea. An Indian superstition claims that ashoka should not be planted near your home; but this is clearly a misunderstanding, since this tree is famous for sheltering women: Buddha's mother held onto an ashoka tree as she gave birth to Buddha, and in the *Ramayana*, an ashoka tree sheltered Sita when she was held captive by Ravana.

Bel, the wood apple tree or Bengal quince, is a fruit-bearing tree that is sacred to Shiva. It has great medicinal virtues for the digestive tract and is used to treat the eyes. Some Vastu texts say that this tree should not be located close to a home. Clearly, fruit trees are beneficial, but some shastra guidelines entreat the reader not to plant this tree close to the house.

Two views of tulsi, or holy basil

Opposite: Set up a dining area in your garden to connect with nature and enjoy relaxed meals outside.

Garden Maintenance

- If you have a compost area, keep it tidy and contained, and do not place it in the northeast.

- Unless you live in an area that has an abundance of rainfall, place attractive jars or barrels to catch the runoff of rain from your roof and store it for the times when there is no rain. Cost-effective gray water and black water systems are now available to route used water from the house to the garden. Most water from the house, providing it contains no toxic chemicals, can benefit the garden instead of being sent back down the drain. Check your local codes to find out if properly treated gray water and black water can be used in your garden. Use natural, nontoxic soaps so that your dishwater, washing machine water, and shower water can help keep your garden going during a dry spell.

- Deadhead flowers. Remove dead debris so that air can flow freely. This clutter-clearing prevents stagnation from developing and revs up the energy of your garden. If plants become sick or infested with insects, take care of the situation right away, both to save the plants and to maintain the most auspicious vibration in your garden.

- Vastu, like many world traditions, recommends picking herbs, fruits, and vegetables in the early morning to harvest their greatest energetic benefit.

- Contemporary fields of knowledge complementary to Vastu indicate that iron and steel gardening implements dry out and deplete the soil, and that copper gardening tools restore and heal the soil. I love using these and recommend them. I offer them for sale through my Web site; see the resource section of this book for more information. These sharp, light tools are based on the research of European Viktor Schauberger, who closely observed nature.

summer. In these days of global warming and increasing droughts, being proactive by harvesting water and planting more trees is a smart, environmentally conscious action in accord with Vastu guidelines.

Attracting birds to your yard is a beneficial influence; it is considered important to do service by feeding others than just yourself. Vastu even has guidelines for the location of domesticated animals. Cows should live in the southeast of the land, horses in the northeast (along with the family's elephants!), and goats in the southwest.

Other Exterior Features

vastu fencing

A fence or compound wall around the rectangle of the property is considered to be auspicious and essential for the health and protection of the inhabitants. This fence should be made of natural materials such as stone, wood, or bamboo. It can also be an attractive boundary hedge created from living shrubs. This wall helps to contain auspicious energies generated by a structure built according to Vastu, as well as the clockwise movement of underground water and other earth energies. To maintain this harmonious effect, the compound wall should be square or rectangular.

rooftop kalash

A *kalash* is a type of finial, an attractive sculptural feature that enhances the life-supporting qualities within your home. Its particular three-dimensional concentric design allows subtle, vibrant cosmic energies to flow into and enliven the building. Depending on the size of your building, you can have one or more *kalashes* on your roof. The main *kalash* should be centered over the *Brahmasthan*. These finials can be made of wood, such as teak, or metal, such as copper, gold, or silver.

wells and water features

The correct placement for a well is in the northeast of your lot, as you may have guessed. North is also a good location for wells and other bodies of water; but for the best effects, do not place them anywhere else. Water storage tanks can be here as well.

If your well is already located in the south, as in the case of one client in India, either close it and drill another in the right sector, or help partially balance its negative influence by enhancing the energy in the north through the addition of a northern fountain or pond.

As discussed in Section Two, all water features are ideally located in the northeast and can also be placed in the north. This applies to ponds, fountains, hot tubs, swimming pools, birdbaths, and all forms of water. Do not, however, place a body of water directly in front of the main entrance to the home.

garage

To have the best Vastu results, the garage or carport should be in the northwest, or even the southeast, and should not be attached to the house. Luckily, detached garages are again the current trend in new construction. If you own an older home in which the garage is located under your bedroom, be sure that the ceiling of the garage is well sealed so that toxic fumes do not enter the bedroom.

Organize your heavy items and storage areas mainly on the west and south walls of the garage rather than the north or east in order to work with the effects of the directions.

Since so many people today enter their homes through their garages, be sure to pay attention to this doorway. I had clients in Vermont who knew that they would always use their attached garage as the main entrance to their home, so we moved this door into an auspicious main door

Vastu for Your Car

Vastu texts describe vehicles and their construction, but most of these guidelines are not useful today. Interestingly, there are prescribed proportions: the classic Vastu text Mayamatam states that the length of the vehicle should be one and a half times the width.

You can add a layer of protection to your vehicle and its occupants with yantras. Install a Sri Yantra transparency on the back windshield and a Narasimha Universal Protection yantra at the top of your front windshield. Use two Universal Protection yantras back-to-back, one facing into the car and one facing outward, or a window transparency decal of this true shield of sacred geometry. The Sri Yantra can be centered directly over the rear light or up at the top of the rear windshield. Mine is low over the rear light, but a friend and I installed the Sri Yantra transparency near the top edge of the windshield in her SUV because she did not want her dogs to drool on it. She loves the uplifting, reassuring presence of the Sri Yantra's goddess energy that she now sees with her rearview mirror. Sri is the goddess Lakshmi, who sends out a constant vibration of health and abundance to those she protects. Lakshmi and yantras are discussed in greater detail in Section Four.

It is valuable to keep your car as clean, fresh, and orderly as your house inside and out. Many people today feel as if they spend as much time in their cars as in their homes, so you might as well make sure that the energetic effect is good. Organize your maps and directions to stores and friends' homes by putting them in a notebook or keeping them clipped together. Empty the trash frequently. This is too small a space to share with debris. On a symbolic level, you don't want to keep carrying your trash or useless reminders of the past with you. Let it go. Watch out that you don't lug around unfinished projects for weeks. Put items in the car to take with you on errands, and then run those errands. Otherwise, these burdens drain you and keep you from feeling relaxed and free.

entry *pada*. This is an example of how we can adapt Vastu guidelines to modern circumstances to help rectify.

If the garage is your main entrance to the home, notice the condition of the door from the garage into the house. Keep it clean, well lighted, and painted. Make some effort to create a pleasing, uplifting entrance, since you see it many times a day. Also, keep the area clear of clutter. It is easy to overlook the importance of this entrance to your home, but attention paid to it will improve how you feel. Have designated places for coats and shoes either near the door to the interior of the house or in a mudroom or other intermediate zone, so that you are not tripping over them or maneuvering through an obstacle course to get into the house. Don't send metaphoric messages to yourself that it is an effort to get home.

When you apply these Vastu guidelines to your home and garden, your sense of happiness, well-being, and inner peace will multiply and your relationships, career, health, and wealth will be supported to blossom even more. Section Four gives even more ways to enhance the energy in your home.

Pools are only located in the northeast or north of the lot. The *yantra* mosaic on the bottom of this swimming pool in Arizona adds greater abundance potency for the household.

more ways to create the transcendental home

I n addition to Vastu, there are many techniques you can use to help rectify spatial energies, increase the supportiveness and health of your home, and create sacred space.

The Power of Meditation

Refined spiritual energy can build up in your home, especially if you are doing spiritual practices such as meditation. These layers of *shakti* make any space feel more sacred and noticeably special. Meditation and other spiritual practices are basic to enhancing energy—they create balance and improve the quality of your home or office. In fact, the best thing you can do besides building according to Vastu to improve the supportiveness of a space is to do spiritual practices (*sadhana*). Prayer, meditation, yoga, chanting, and breathing practices (*pranayama*) all enliven a space. Visitors will notice and comment on how good your home feels. I have had this happen over and over for years. Several acquaintances, because they have felt that my home was tranquil and energetically

Meditation makes everything

come alive.

—Sri Sri Ravi Shankar

special, were inspired to begin Sahaj Samadhi Meditation and Sudarshan Kriya, practical techniques taught through the Art of Living Foundation.

Be consistent with the spiritual practices of whatever tradition you are drawn to. As the Sufi poet Rumi said, your true home is within and reachable by letting go and allowing the mind to go inward. When we feel at home within ourselves and within our own hearts, any building we live in will feel more serene and supportive. Meditation practices make us more perceptive of our environment, so that we intuitively know many of the changes to make. We become more in touch, literally and metaphorically.

Traditionally, there are over a hundred ways to meditate. Here are a few methods that bring you back to your Self. In the first, use the power of memory to remember very positive moments from the past. Sit quietly and bring your awareness to those happy times; your whole being will get into that state of joy and evenness.

Another meditation can be done when you are near a quickly moving mountain stream, perhaps one with waterfalls, or in your home at an indoor waterfall that you have installed in the north-east sector. Just observe the flow of the water and allow it to wash your mind clean, to clear out any stress and worries that weigh you down. Go with the flow, and let go. This easy technique is described in ancient Vedic writings known as *shastras*.

Within you there is a stillness

and a sanctuary to which you

can retreat at any time and

be yourself.

—HERMANN HESSE, *SIDDHARTHA*

Love and Devotion

Everyone knows how we feel transformed and lit up when we are in love. All of our cells vibrate with love energy. Love's power affects the environment as well. Loving and tending to your home and workspace enliven and heal those spaces. I had taken this for granted but got a clear demonstration of it when staying in the guesthouse of a friend's property that was on the market. The main house had been vacant for many months. I used its kitchen and a few other parts of the house but didn't strongly connect with it. I burned sage in the house and aired it out since it had felt a bit creepy when I arrived, and I was relieved at the results. But when a house-hunting couple, in their own words, fell in love with the house, the entire feeling level changed. The house was so happy to feel appreciated and loved that it responded by being an infinitely more lively and pleasant space to be.

You can give loving attention to your own home in many ways: appreciating everything you have and the value of those things in your life, keeping the house clean and decorating it, and using Vastu guidelines to enhance its health and energy.

Likewise, your good intentions, love, prayer, meditation, and sincere devotion can help transcend obstacles and rules. This doesn't mean that the Vastu rules are not in effect but that the result of violating certain guidelines can be softened. The absolute best situation is to live in a house designed according to Vastu with *Ayadi* calculations—and to do regular meditation and spiritual practices.

Watching koi in a beautiful pond, such as this one at Sunrise Springs in Santa Fe, calms the mind and brings you into communion with nature and your true self.

Leaving Shoes at the Door

To improve the general energy of your home, adopt the intelligent Asian habit of leaving shoes by the entry. This keeps the dirt and stress of the everyday world outside of your space, setting it apart as quieter, cleaner, more sacred, and more peaceful. You will feel the difference and hopefully will choose to maintain the practice. This will also aid your feeling of groundedness and connection to the earth, since your feet will be directly in touch with the floor (which is hopefully a natural material). If I leave my shoes on all the time, I feel more worn out and tense at the end of the day and my feet feel uncomfortably tingly and stressed. There is clearly a relaxing, healing, more settled feeling in my nervous system when I remove my shoes when indoors.

Since one of the pathways the body uses to clear stress out of the system is through the feet, shoes tend to collect that energy. This is another reason to go barefoot when you can and give your feet a breathing break. When you can, walk directly on the earth as well. Many texts recommend walking on the dewy grass in the morning—a beautiful practice that helps reestablish the healthy connection with the natural elements that we were intended to have. When the weather permits, try this. You may notice increased ease and breathe a sigh of relief.

Organizing/Clearing Clutter

Keeping your space clean, orderly, and free of clutter also greatly enhances the sacredness of the energy. You've experienced that a noticeable sparkle comes into a space when it is cleaned. Part of this results from the greater freshness and purity. In addition, the power of your attention tangibly revs up the vibrational effect of the room. Sometimes my clients want help organizing and clearing clutter in their homes. One Boulder client reported that "with this cleansing process, it just feels better and better each day." She began to feel more in control of her life, had greater clarity, and felt less overwhelmed. She found more time to take care of herself and to take action on projects, since she was, as she put it, less in her own way. Very soon after this process, she acknowledged and acted upon her longtime secret dream of becoming a massage therapist. She now radiates greater happiness and fulfillment. This client also experienced greater ease from knowing where to locate resources she already had in her home. Weeding out useless and outdated items allows you to access what you already have but couldn't see or find before. Organizing allows you to reclaim your own space and your own self, to reconstruct your own center from inside your home.

An important aspect of the damaging effect of clutter is summed up in the Indian aphorism, "Unfinished projects drain your energy." You have probably noticed this and also the great relief and feeling of freedom that comes over you when you complete some dreaded or long-delayed task. Piles of paper on your desk or on the floor lead to debilitating feelings of being overwhelmed and anxious.

Forget not that the earth delights in your bare feet and the winds want to play with your hair.

—KAHLIL GIBRAN

Organizing these amorphous towers of confusion enables you to find things quickly and easily. It is self-empowering and increases self-confidence. If you need help doing this, enlist a friend.

Boxes of uncompleted projects and unwanted household items in your home or office create an unsettled, cluttered, temporary feeling. Don't remain in this ungrounded state, unable to move forward. Once you move into a space, unpack! Fully settle into your new home or office space.

A client in New Jersey wrote me, saying:

I cleaned up a very chaotic area in the kitchen—piles of paper, lots of things that didn't belong there, junk mail—and replaced it with a beautiful ceramic tray, vase of flowers, and two round rattan bowls for all the incoming mail and the day planner. Just like you predicted, it made us feel so

much lighter. That night during dinner my husband commented on how fresh the room felt, how enjoyable it was to look at, and how it really affects our well-being. The whole weekend I felt light and uplifted from changing these areas. The whole energy shifted in the kitchen. It is so peaceful. Even the unseen affected us: when we cleaned up cabinets and drawers that were hidden from the eye, the effect was profound because it uncluttered our own being as well as the physical space.

Indeed, my own experience, like that of my clients', is that organizing your closets and drawers will clear your mind and ground your emotions. Just making these small decisions, weeding out useless items, and reorganizing what you store there will affect you and the entire home. As Gaston Bachelard put it in *The Poetics of Space*, "In the wardrobe there exists a center of order that protects the entire house against uncurbed disorder."[1]

Laundry: What to Do with Dirty Clothes

Do not place laundry baskets in the center or the northeast of any room in your home; these are sacred areas that should be kept clean and fresh. An easy, convenient system to deal with this ongoing issue of dirty clothes is to invest in a large, beautiful woven basket with a lid. That way your soiled clothes are in a breathable container that hides them and at the same time becomes an attractive feature that you won't mind seeing. If you're used to open plastic baskets or metal and cloth sorting racks, get several baskets with lids, perhaps of varying sizes, for your dark load, white load, and handwashable items. Having open laundry bins means that you are continuously being reminded that your work is never done and that your home seems to be perpetually dirty and disorderly.

Aromatherapy

Use natural air fresheners instead of products that use artificial scents—these toxic, dead substances deplete *prana*. Used in moderation, high-quality incense purifies the air and creates an atmosphere of spirituality, richness, and sensory pleasure. It is worth adopting the Japanese and Chinese tradition of "listening to incense" rather than just smelling it. This is an excellent meditative ritual of stopping the mind by being fully with what is happening, truly noticing the incense burning as a special event rather than thinking about many things at once, as we usually do. This is one of many techniques you can use to bring your mind to the present moment.

Most of the best incense comes from Japan and India. Select incense that is made from natural ingredients like herbs, resins, and wood. Some incense includes synthetic ingredients that are toxic and defeat the purpose of using incense in the first place.

Another option is burning camphor, a natural substance derived from a type of cinnamon tree. Camphor traditionally symbolizes purity and creates a calming effect. However, be careful that the camphor you purchase is natural, since most camphor that is sold today is synthetic and will not have the effect and benefits of the tree resin.

Also valuable are ritual aromatic purification substances of the Americas. Try Native American remedies: sage sticks clear out negative energies, and burning sweetgrass braids brings in positive energies. You can experiment with several kinds of smudge sticks, such as white sage, mountain sage, and *yerba santa*. Copal is a resin obtained from trees that has both medicinal and spiritual effects. There are several types of copal available that have slightly different energies.

You can set the intention to cleanse and enliven your home and then walk clockwise around the space with these substances. Open all the windows for fresh air and take fire-safety precautions by holding a bowl underneath your incense or sage.

Judicious use of pure organic essential oils fills the air with soothing or exhilarating scents. Essential oils purify the air and kill harmful bacteria, mold, and viruses; they also balance emotions. Put essential oils on cotton balls to scent an area or diffuse them into the air to heal and transform. You can put a few drops of essential oils in your humidifier or pour in a little pesticide-free true rosewater. Be sure to read the instructions for your humidifier before doing this, since it can damage some humidifiers.

Room sprays with essential oils can be used for space clearing or blessing and enlivening your home. Vetiver is an earthy, soothing oil that can be used in the southwest for grounding. Sandalwood and peppermint are both cooling and have other beneficial properties. Peppermint is refreshing; sandalwood is considered both a spiritual scent and an aphrodisiac. In India, a traditional way to cool off during hot weather is to put moistened, ground sandalwood paste on your forehead. You can burn sandalwood incense or wood chips or diffuse the essential oil.

Air Quality

Indoor air quality is frequently much worse than outdoor air quality. Air pollution decreases the amount of *soma*, the lunar energy component of *prana*, in the air. This imbalance and depletion of a subtle energy that we all need is one of the reasons that today's cities are agitating and deplete our energy and sense of calm. Since city air is deficient in these soothing, nourishing qualities, we need the tranquility and harmony that result from Vastu even more.

Make sure you have some fresh air coming into your home and your workspace. Many buildings were built airtight, so fresh air does not enter. Often the buildings themselves are toxic because of the building materials used. Use air purifiers to help clear pollutants. Change the filter in your furnace frequently to save energy and breathe more easily.

Salt, baking soda (bicarbonate of soda), and talcum powder can clear out some levels of yucky energy. Put these white powders in paper cups in the corners of the rooms. After 24 hours, throw out the cups and whatever they have absorbed. A client who used this technique in a rented art studio reported that she was amazed at how much better and less oppressive it felt after she followed my recommendation with salt and baking soda.

Healthy plants rev up the energy and add beauty and oxygen to your environment. Every home and workspace should have some plants to sparkle up the atmosphere. Houseplants are perfectly in compliance with Vastu and have a powerful effect that creates greater happiness, ease, life-energy, and beauty. In general, avoid milky-sapped and thorny plants, as in your garden. Some plants have a greater ability than others to detoxify the air in your home or office. There are claims that *tulsi* and orchids add more oxygen to the environment than other plants. In addition, *tulsi* plants purify the air. Having plants in your home connects you to the vibrancy of nature. If you are not good with plants, consider taking a workshop at your local nursery or hiring someone to maintain your plants. You can also add this healthy, nourishing effect by having fresh flowers in your home. Even a single blossom in a vase will enliven a room and bring nurturing beauty to your life.

Lighting

Light sources should be as natural as possible. In the Vedic tradition, the seven major visible wavelengths of light are perceived as *devas*, impulses of creative intelligence, whose nourishing influences bless our lives. They are the seven horses that power the chariot of *Surya*, the sun: violet, indigo, blue, green, yellow, orange, and red. The invisible but well-known rays of infrared and ultra violet are part of this group and bring the number of rays to nine. Some amount of each is vital to health.

I recommend using full-spectrum light bulbs to improve the uplifting and nourishing qualities of light in your space. They cost a little more but last much longer and come close to imitating the full range of sunlight. A friend who lives in a garden level condo had complained that his home was depressing and dark; once he switched to using full spectrum light bulbs in his light fixtures, he reported feeling happier and more clear.

This is especially important because we spend so many hours indoors. SAD (Seasonal Affective Disorder) is a form of depression caused by decreased exposure to sunshine during winter months. Sunlight is necessary to health. Special lights that imitate nature by emitting more of a

More and more, it seems to me, light is the beautifier of the building.

—FRANK LLOYD WRIGHT

full spectrum are beneficial for everyone. Having windows and openings on the east and north allows healing light to enter our homes and offices, but it is usually not enough illumination for all of our needs.

Artificial lighting that is not full-spectrum creates an unhealthy effect on our bodies, minds, and emotions. Studies show that people tend to be more depressed, tired, cloudy-minded, and prone to illness when exposed to the fluorescent lighting that is prevalent in offices and schools. Many people are so used to being disconnected from nature that they do not notice this, but it has a palpable effect that seriously restricts student learning and job productivity in the work world. There are full-spectrum fluorescent tubes available that are better than ordinary fluorescents. Getting rid of fluorescent lighting can make your body and mind drop a burden of stress and tension that you may not have even been aware of.

Some candles, especially paraffin ones, contain lead or other toxic ingredients. In addition to being aesthetically pleasing and naturally fragrant, beeswax candles produce negative ions when burning, thus producing an even healthier, more relaxing environment. Negative ions are high by waterfalls and the ocean; they are practically non-existent in most modern, sealed-up office buildings.

Artwork

Having all of your walls vacant can create a sterile feeling and make life feel lonely and unsettled. Place something on the walls and around your home—art and ornaments that you find uplifting and beautiful. Remember that what you put your attention on grows stronger in your life. War, violence, misery, and depressing scenes are not supportive for the home as healing sanctuary; these subjects can be powerful social commentary in art but are better suited for places other than your home. Avoid harsh, jagged images that seem to attack. Look for art that expands and enlivens your soul and consciousness, not just your intellect. *Mayamata* recommends putting paintings on interior and exterior walls, specifically "joyous scenes and religious images."[2]

You may have read in some Feng Shui books that abstract art is not a good influence, but this is a misunderstanding. Having beautiful, high-quality abstract art in your home will not weaken it or yourself with amorphous, unfinished qualities. Instead, abstract art can enliven you and your home with uplifting, energizing, peaceful influences of color and subtle vibrational energies.

As an artist myself, I am acutely aware of the effect of art. Art should enliven and expand consciousness, energy, joy, and serenity for the artist and the viewer. Swami Muktananda says, "The artist must always be responsible for what he brings into the world; he must always paint the highest. As well as acting as receivers of energy, the *chakras* also transmit energy, as do works of art."[3]

These yantras were created with colored pigments on sand.

Yantras: Cosmic Diagrams

Yantras are beautiful, geometrically precise diagrams with symbolic meaning and potent vibrational energy. They are the original sacred geometry and are from India's ancient Vedic tradition. *Yantras* are also exquisite pieces of art that pulsate with healing magic. As a technology of the sacred, they generate nourishing, life-enhancing energy fields and rectify dissonant spatial energies, both inner and outer. *Yantras* are archetypal images that create sacred space; they embody cosmic divine energies, the Pure Being that we are, radiating into the physical world in which we dwell.

Proper placement of *yantras* is another level of acknowledging and honoring the forces of nature. The impulses of the directions, elements, deities, and planets exert powerful but subtle vibratory effects on our bodies, minds, and emotions. *Yantras* can help us be in tune with nature so that we have the support of nature rather than the experience of resistance from nature. *Yantras* are used in the construction of temples to potentize and to connect with divine principles and energies. They are placed underneath the central *pada* of the temple's *garbha-griha* and at other specific points of the building, including behind some of the sculpture. There are also *yantras* that are used for particular ceremonies and *yantras* that can be used in your home and office. Their sacred symbolism can be constructed on the floor or a wall, incised on metal such as copper or gold, inscribed on rock crystal, or drawn or printed on paper. The free *yantra* guidebook on my Web site gives detailed information for further study; see the resource section of this book for more information.

shri yantra

Shri Yantra.

"Shri" in Sanskrit is Lakshmi or opulent wealth. (You may also see it transliterated as "Shree" and "Sri," but they are all pronounced the same way.) Often called the greatest yantra, the Shri Yantra represents Shri Lakshmi, the Feminine Divine form of the flow of all aspects of abundance. Installing a Shri Yantra in your home or car is an excellent way to bring in goddess energy to support and bless your life and space. Contemporary American artist Bill Witherspoon has experimented with the creation of large-scale earthworks of the Shri Yantra and found that soil became richer and more productive, so this yantra has powerful applications for your garden as well.

The Shri Yantra represents the creative unfolding and expansion of the manifest universe from its source, represented by the *bindu* point in the center of the Shri Yantra. It depicts the union of the Masculine and Feminine Divine, or integration of cosmic principles, which can be perceived as Shiva and Shakti or as Vishnu and Lakshmi. It is also viewed as the embodiment of the Feminine Divine in the form of Shri Lakshmi (abundance) and Tripura Sundari (beauty). The Shri Yantra can be used in many situations in your home, such as on the front door for a general blessing and protection.

The three-dimensional form of the Shri Yantra is known as a Meru Chakra or Shri Chakra. This *yantra* resembles a mountain in its shape and has also been part of the Vedic tradition for thousands of years. Since it is three-dimensional instead of just two-dimensional, it is even more potent.

planetary yantras

As mentioned in Section Two, you can bring your home more in tune with nature through the Vedic astrological tradition of Jyotish. Each of the eight directions has a planetary lord assigned from the nine *grahas* or celestial luminaries. Just as the sun and the moon have profound influences on the growth of plants, the oceans, and our own bodies, so do the planets. Unless you are living in a Vastu house designed with *Ayadi* calculations, being in a new architectural space is like getting a second astrological chart imposed upon you. This can lead to alterations in your finances, health, relationships, and other areas of life. You have probably noticed that sometimes people experience big changes in their lives after moving to a new house or adding on to their existing home. If there are defects in the structure of your house—ways in which it deviates from Vastu guidelines—there is a corresponding weakening of the planet, its range of influence, and effects.

Since the *grahas* serve as planetary lords of the directions, this gives us another tool for improving the energy of our homes and other buildings. If there is a need for strengthening or honoring of a direction's energy, install the *yantra* for that planet. These *yantras* can also be used to help become friends with the planets in your astrological chart or to aid during difficult planetary transits. There

Eighteenth-century crystal yantra, Nepal.

Gold Meru Chakra, the three-dimensional
form of the Shri Yantra.

are many properties, roles, and areas of life affected by these planetary regents. Here is a brief primer on planetary *yantras* that have developed over millennia. For additional detailed information, see the resource section of this book. I use what I consider to be the most accurate correspondence of planets and chakras of the human body, which was developed in consultation with several Vedic scholars. If you intuitively feel you should place the yantras differently, trust yourself.

I explain the planetary yantras beginning from the northeast, moving clockwise, and finishing with the north, which is how I would proceed if I were installing all of these planetary yantras in your home. The northeast is the sacred zone where we lay the cornerstone and begin work on a building, and beneficial earth energies move in a clockwise direction.

Guru/Jupiter and *Ketu*/south node of the moon. In the case of the important northeast sector, there are two planets, Jupiter as the primary lord and Ketu as secondary lord. These can be used with a blocked northeast, a northeast bathroom, or other structural weaknesses in this sector. Place the Ketu yantra on the wall at the height of the crown of your head. The Jupiter yantra is assigned to the second or spleen chakra, which is above the genitals and below the navel.

Surya/Sun. East is ruled by the sun, which rises from that direction. If the east of your home is closed and has no windows or doors to let in the beneficial energies and light of the sun, adding a *Surya* yantra can help. Place it at the height of your third eye, the sixth chakra, which is located in between the eyebrows.

Shukra/Venus. The southeast has the planet Venus for its regent. If your building has a southeast extension, you can place the Venus yantra as a partial remedy at the height of your heart or fourth chakra. If you sleep in the southeast sector and have no way of moving your bedroom to another room, install the Venus yantra under the mattress, facing upward.

Mangal/Mars. Mars rules the southern direction. If you have a very exposed southern side of your dwelling or have a southern entrance in an inauspicious *pada*, it is beneficial to install a Mars yantra. Place it at the height of your solar plexus or third chakra, about two inches above your navel.

Rahu/north node of the moon. The southwest is ruled by Rahu. If the southwest of your home or office is not designed or utilized properly, one partial remedy is to install a Rahu yantra at the level of the base of your spine, the first or root chakra.

Shani/Saturn. The planetary ruler of the west is Saturn. If your building has defects in the west, such as lots of windows, you can install a Saturn yantra, perhaps as a transparent decal on the window, to help deflect any negative influence. The root or first chakra, at the level of the base of your spine, is the correct placement for a Saturn yantra.

Shukra/Venus yantra.

Chandra/Moon. Northwest is the realm of the moon. If the northwest, which is air element, is stuffy and has inadequate air flow, use a moon yantra at the height of your third eye, just between the eyebrows, the sixth chakra. In addition, open a window to bring fresh air into the house.

Budha/Mercury. The north is ruled by Mercury, which supports communication. Heavy items in the north instead of the south or west can weaken Mercury, as can a lack of windows or doors in the north. Using the color green and installing a Mercury yantra at the height of your throat, the fifth chakra, can help alleviate these debilitating structural problems.

Another tool for spatial energies in buildings that were not designed as Vastu structures is a Vedic Pyramid, which includes all nine of the planetary yantras. It is a contemporary combination of detailed layers of vibrational space-healing energy, including glass pyramids that sparkle in the light, color planetary direction yantras under each pyramid, auspicious mantras, and the *Vastu Purusha Mandala*. Its gold plating covers five metals in a traditional formula—silver, antimony, copper, zinc, and pewter—that amplifies the energy transmitted into its environment.

pranapratishtha: *yantra* installation and activation

Pranapratishtha has been described as breathing life energy or *prana* into the *yantra* so that it becomes alive and vibrantly supports you by emitting specific nourishing vibrations into the environment. The energies are already there in the *yantra*, but this honoring ritual wakes them up and helps focus our intention. If the *yantra*'s measurements are custom designed for you using *Ayadi* calculations, it will be even more potent and vibrant.

Traditionally there are various chants and ritual performances for *pranapratishtha*. Even without these time-tested elements, you can enliven your home by designing your own ceremony, if it comes from the heart and is supported by your own clear intention, what in Sanskrit is called *sankalpa*. You can write out your desires for health, happiness, and abundance to read or offer during your ritual. Prepare for your ceremony by cleaning the house and taking a shower. If you wish, you may ring a bell to start your ceremony and clear the air. Ritual offerings of fruit, flowers, incense, and water can also be part of *pranapratishtha*. Trust yourself to develop your own ritual, or follow the instructions provided with the *yantras*.

Madhu Khanna defines *pranapratishtha* as "the infusing of vital force (*prana*) into the geometrical pattern of the yantra." She explains that "the yantra ... becomes a radiant emblem and receptacle of cosmic power (*shakti-rūpa*) and consciousness (*chaitanya*) transforming into sacred archetypal space."[4] One of the processes she describes is "'fencing the quarters' (*digbandhana*)," which is performed "by snapping . . . [your] right thumb and middle finger ten times (8 points of the compass + nadir + zenith)."[5] Here again we see the importance of acknowledging the cardinal directions of north, south, east, and west, and the intermediate directions, northeast, southeast, southwest, and northwest.

Budha/Mercury yantra.

Sound: Music and *Mantras*

We have all noticed the clear and palpable value of uplifting happy music such as "Zip-A-Dee-Doo-Dah" or the "Hallelujah" chorus. Obviously any music that expands the heart improves inner and outer space. How can you not feel light and joyful when hearing Sinatra sing "I've Got the World on a String?" Music of this nature enhances the qualities we all want in our homes.

Music has a mathematical basis and is one of the fields of Vastu knowledge. I am researching CDs created specifically according to Vastu guidelines and hope to make them available. In the meantime, I have found a wonderful *Sri Yantra* CD that was constructed mathematically as a sound equivalent of the Shri Yantra; many people find that they and their environment are brought into greater balance by the healing, meditative effect of this CD. I recommend three more excellent CDs for helping to create the transcendental home. *Sacred Chants of Shiva* and *Sacred Chants of Devi* bring deep silence and purity; in addition, the mantra chants on these CDs add a vibration of healing delicacy. *Vastu-Purusha, Harmony of Space* is another excellent CD that includes chants to Vastu Purusha and the planetary lords of the directions. All four of these CDs are available on my Web site.

> Music is the divine way to tell beautiful, poetic things to the heart.
>
> —Pablo Casals

mantras

Mantras are Sanskrit sound vibrations that have a positive effect on the environment. Mantras heal inner and outer space. They are absorbed into the air when chanted. Some mantras are used silently for meditation, leading the mind inward to its source. The mantra *Om* is a potent mantra but is only used out loud. As a mantra for silent meditation, *Om* is only appropriate and beneficial for celibates in retreat from the world, not those of us living an integrated, active life.

There are mantras associated with most yantras, which increase their effect. Mantras can be used as sacred vibrational blessings for your home. Sri Sri Ravi Shankar has called the chanting of mantras "the ancient technique of recharging the environment with pure vibrations." There are frequently a number of alternate mantras for the same purpose, including for honoring planetary influences, so you can choose the one that you are most drawn to. You may also write your own prayers, rituals of intention, and honoring ceremonies for use in your home, business, and garden. All sincere expressions are effective.

Traditional Vastu mantra to honor and enliven your home:

दिग्दोषनाशकयन्त्र

Oṁ mahābhāgavatāya vāstupuruṣāya svāhā.

Om. To the great adorable lord, the soul of the dwelling, we consecrate the offering.

Honored guests should always be greeted with a warm welcome. This mantra acknowledges and supports Vastu Purusha, the transcendental soul of your home.

Vāstoshpati Sūkta, *Rig Veda*, Seventh Mandala, Hymn 54, Invocation for the Home:

Guardian of the house, welcome us.
Be a good place, free of disease.
Fulfill the desires that we ask for.
Give peace and happiness to the people and animals that dwell here.

Protector-Parent of the Home, as a form of Soma,
Allow us to flourish, increasing our knowledge, abundance, and energy.
Through loving friendship with you and in your enfolding guardianship
May we be ever-youthful.

Protector of our house, our well-being is enhanced by your dear companionship.
May we gain success and happy progress through your harmony and strength.
Provide what is best for us during work and during rest.
May all divine energies be auspicious to us always with blessings.[6]

This is traditionally a blessing for a new home, but it can be used at any time.

A blessing from *Katha Upanishad* for your home.

Saha nav avatu
Saha nau bhunaktu
Saha viryam karavāvahai
Tejasvi nav adhitam astu
Ma vidvishāvahai

Let us be together
Let us eat together
Let us be vital together
Let us be radiating truth, radiating the light of life
Never shall we denounce anyone, never entertain negativity.

Speaking harshly, speaking against others, dwelling on the negative, and complaining drag down your energy and radiate that effect into your environment. Whatever you focus on grows stronger in your life. Take a vow to yourself to bring mindfulness to this. Do not force negativity from your mind or try to push it away; this would be counterproductive, since forcing the mind works against nature, not with it. Allow these behaviors to drop from your life over time by observing what is happening in the mind and letting it go.

Another useful awareness exercise is to observe how you feel when listening to complaints and negativity from others. Close your eyes and notice what's happening inside of you. Do this also when listening to a friend's enthusiasm and happiness. Observe the effect. You can practice this process on your own as well: Think of someone you dislike. Notice how this makes you feel. Then think of someone you really love. Notice any emotions coming up or physical sensations in the body. Does your chest tighten? Does your breathing change?

Sacred Archetypal Energies

Sacred archetypal energies are embodied in some wonderful aspects of the masculine and feminine divine that radiate a beautiful influence into the environment. These archetypes represent qualities we all wish to exemplify. India, even before the Hindu religion, perceived a three-fold Masculine Divine known as Brahma, Vishnu, and Shiva. Brahma is the creator or generator, Vishnu is the maintainer or operator, and Shiva is the destroyer or transformer, pure transcendental consciousness. Mayan, the founder of Vastu, describes all three of these as aspects of the center of each subtle cube of energy, which, when honored in architectural design, is Vastu made manifest in the living organism of your home.

There are also myriad aspects of Devi, the Feminine Divine. From one perspective, Devi is more powerful and comes before all the others. When negative forces cannot be overcome, she easily handles the situation.

The stories of these sacred archetypal energies are inspirational and can be thought of as myths to guide us in the experience of life. You may choose to incorporate their images in your home, or you may find others that hold meaning for you.

Opposite: This beautiful Indian miniature painting captures the movement within transcendental silence and grace that exemplifies Shiva. Eighteenth-century gouache on paper, Pahari School, Seu-Nainsukh family. Calcutta, Indian Museum.

shiva

Shiva is the transformer and destroyer. The old state must be cleared away before the new one can arise. Shiva is also translated as innocence, transcendence, and purity. Vastu recognizes Shiva as dancing in the center of the space at a subtle level.

Shiva Mantra:

Om namah shivaya.

This is one of the oldest and most beneficial mantras.

shri lakshmi

This goddess' name explains her popularity. "Sri" means "flow of wealth" in Sanskrit. The word derivation of "Lakshmi" has to do with taking aim and hitting the target, as in archery. Since Lakshmi is the goddess of wealth and prosperity, good luck and good fortune, she certainly is welcome. There are traditionally *ashtalakshmi*, eight forms of Lakshmi, eight aspects of her bounty: the wealth of spiritual knowledge, financial prosperity, fame, health, the wealth of love-relationship-family life, success-victory in your actions, abundance of food and nourishment for life, and courage-integrity-character. There are several versions of these eight aspects of Lakshmi. These provide an abundance of ways in which to be wealthy, since the lists can be consolidated and total much more than eight in number! My compilation overflows into nine.

Adhi Lakshmi is the first or original aspect, the inner wealth of spiritual knowledge and enlightenment, sometimes referred to as Vidya Lakshmi, "knowledge." In a talk about the eight forms of Lakshmi that I attended in Bangalore in 1991, Sri Sri Ravi Shankar said: "Knowledge of the source is the first and biggest wealth. The grace of Adhi Lakshmi means 'one who is aware of one's source.' "

Vijaya Lakshmi is the wealth of success. With the blessings of Vijaya Lakshmi, you are always victorious; whatever you do is successful.

Powerful Veera Lakshmi brings the energy of abundant courage—fiery, powerful—into your life.

Raja Lakshmi is the wealth of authority and political power. This aspect of Lakshmi has also been described as Aishwarya Lakshmi: the great fortune of brilliance and splendor, supremacy and royal power. Raja Lakshmi includes supernatural powers or *siddhis*, natural human abilities that most of us do not seem to have.

Gaja Lakshmi, fame, is a form of wealth that we can be graced with, although it doesn't necessarily mean success in all areas of life. People can be famous for their creative work but not have money; for example, sometimes movie stars have Gaja Lakshmi (fame) and Dhana Lakshmi (financial abundance), but they may lack some other kind of abundance.

Santhana Lakshmi is the wealth of having children, family, or other loved ones. Having caring people around you—true friends who are the family of your heart and soul, whether or not they are related by blood—is a form of abundance to be treasured.

Bhagya Lakshmi personifies the riches of good health, which gives us the ability to enjoy all the blessings that are available to us in this life without restriction.

Dhanya Lakshmi is the goddess representing the abundance of grains and other wonderful foods, and of having enough fresh food to eat.

Eightfold Lakshmi.

Dhana Lakshmi is the aspect of Lakshmi that is most well known and worshipped: money. She is the abundance of financial prosperity that is chased after with such determination on this planet. Dhana Lakshmi offers us the freedom to enjoy and participate in a wide range of richness of experience beyond mere survival.

Sri Sri gives the following advice for enhancing abundance: "Whatever you have increases in life. Feel the plenty. Instead of saying it could be less, say it could be more. 'I would like to have this' is better than saying 'I don't have this.' It is a shift of consciousness. Don't be in lack consciousness. Then your attention is in a positive direction."

If you would like an image of Lakshmi in your home, choose one in which she is seated rather than standing. Symbolically, the seated position indicates a stronger, more accomplished acquisition of the abundance we all desire in our lives. Of course, any artwork you bring into your life should be something that you find truly pleasing.

Lakshmi mantras:

Om shrim klim lakshmi narayana-bhyam namaha.

This mantra acknowledges both Lakshmi and her male counterpart, Narayana. Lakshmi is actually pronounced in Sanskrit something like "luck" and is the source of that English word. Narayana is the Sanskrit source of our English "nervous system." Integrating the flow of all eight aspects of Lakshmi's luck-abundance with our own nervous system would be supreme prosperity.

Om shrim namaha.

This Lakshmi mantra honors the Feminine Divine's flow of wealth in our lives on all levels.

ganesha

Ganesha, also known as Ganesh, Ganaraya, and Ganapati, is saluted at the start of new projects. As the remover of obstacles, he is an excellent friend. He also is considered a guardian figure, the par excellence protector of women. Many homes place an image of Ganesha at the front door for protection. Ganapati has another secret meaning in Vastu. *Gana* in Sanskrit means "measure or mathematics." *Pati* means "lord." So Ganesha, or Ganapati, is integrally a part of the Vastu tradition, which uses precise mathematics to create buildings that are living organisms.

Ganesha mantra:

Om gam ganapataye namah

He is a man of sense who does not grieve for what he has not, but rejoices in what he has.

—Epictetus, First-Century Greek Philosopher

Ganesha, the remover of obstacles and protector of women. Twenty-first century Bengali Patua painting.

Grace and Gratitude

Gratitude increases all aspects of abundance and joy in life. Observe the mind when it is complaining. How do your body and emotions feel when you complain? Is this self-inflicted effect something that you want in your life? Remember all the blessings in your life. Observe how you feel when you focus on the positive. This feeling level is projected into your environment and back onto you again.

Whatever you put your attention on grows stronger in your life.

You may find it valuable to make a list of everything that has happened in the last year that you are grateful for: growth in inner being, financial success, career breakthroughs, health improvements, everything. Make another list of what you want to accomplish and receive in the upcoming year. Offer them both up to nature or the divine or your higher self. You can do this at the beginning of each month on the day of the new moon, each season on the solstice or equinox, or at the new year.

These awareness exercises will improve the quality of your inner and outer environment. They enhance the flow of grace, which will make you and your architectural space both feel better and be more supported. Like meditation, they can help rectify negative influences, thus making your built space an even more nourishing and harmonious environment.

Section Four has offered a diverse range of tips to increase the positive energy and peace within our homes. We can transform our current homes into transcendental homes by utilizing these inner and outer remedies to support the application of Vastu design.

Vastu: Creating the Transcendental Home, Being in Harmony with Nature

Vastu brings harmony, balance, and well-being to your living space and thus to your life. Just knowing about the powerful, sacred knowledge from this tradition creates a purifying, strengthening effect on the individual and the environment. Implementing Vedic knowledge transforms us and heals our surroundings even more than just reading about it. When you are ready, buying appropriate land and building with Vastu will be an excellent investment in your quality of life. In the meantime, use Vastu to bring your home into greater alignment with nature through the suggestions presented here.

Creating a transcendental home through Vastu provides the base from which we can have happier, healthier, more successful lives, in spite of stress and uncertainty on our beautiful planet. My wish for us all is that we use this great opportunity to transform our homes into oases of tranquility

When there is gratitude, complaints disappear. When complaints arise, gratitude disappears. When there is a complaint in the mind, there is discontent, frustration, dejection, depression. This is the lower journey. Gratitude is the plateau, the middle. When you rise above that, there is grace. When gratitude in you stays, that very gratitude flows out from you as grace.

—Sri Sri Ravi Shankar

and abundance in harmony with nature. May we become a source of healing and light for ourselves, the environment, and the world.

It's time to start

living the life

you've imagined.

—Henry James

Courtesy of Marpa Design Studio.

Sunrise Springs, Santa Fe

Section V

resources

Resources for More Knowledge

how to contact the author

Sherri Silverman

Transcendence Design

P.O. Box 2461

Santa Fe, NM 87504

http://transcendencedesign.com

Design consultations for home, garden, and business spaces. Yantras, incense, CDs, home furnishings, garden products, and conscious natural lifestyle products. Visit www.transcendencedesign.com/events/ for information on book signings and events in your area.

Note: Information on Vastu and the Southern Hemisphere will be posted on the author's Web site.

books

Vastu

Sthapati, Ganapati. *Building Architecture of Sthapatya Veda*. Chennai, India: Dakshinaa Publishing House, 2001. All of Sthapati's books are recommended. This is the main compendium.

India's Home Décor Craft Traditions

More information on the practice of decorating the threshold of the home:

Fisher, Nora, ed. *Mud, Mirror, and Thread: Folk Traditions of Rural India*. Middletown, NJ: Grantha/Santa Fe: Museum of New Mexico Press/Ahmedabad, India: Mapin, 1993.

Huyler, Stephen P. *Painted Prayers: Women's Art in Village India*. New York: Rizzoli, 1994.

Natural House Construction and Design

Alexander, Jane. *The Illustrated Spirit of the Home: How to Make Your Home a Sanctuary*. London: Thorsons/HarperCollins, 1999.

Baker-Laporte, Paula, Erica Elliott, M.D., and John Banta. *Prescriptions for a Healthy House: A Practical Guide for Architects, Builders and Homeowners*. Vancouver, B.C.: New Society Publishers, 2001.

Baker-Laporte, Paula and Robert Laporte. *Econest: Creating Sustainable Sanctuaries of Clay, Straw, and Timber*. Layton, UT: Gibbs Smith, 2005.

Spiritual Gardening

Mosko, Martin Hakubai ASLA and Alxe Noden. *Landscape as Spirit: Creating a Contemplative Garden*. Trumbull, CT: Weatherhill, 2003.

Streep, Peg. *Spiritual Gardening: Creating Sacred Space Outdoors*. Hawaii: Inner Ocean, 1999.

Sound and *Mantra*

Ashley-Farrand, Thomas. *Healing Mantras: Using Sound Affirmations for Personal Power, Creativity, and Healing*. New York: Ballantine Wellspring/Random House, 1999.

Berendt, Joachim-Ernst. *Nada Brahma: The World Is Sound, Music and The Landscape of Consciousness*. Rochester, VT: Destiny Books/Inner Traditions, 1987.

Paul, Russill. *The Yoga of Sound: Healing and Enlightenment Through the Sacred Practice of Mantra*. Novato, CA: New World Library, 2003.

Yantras

Khanna, Madhu. *Yantra: The Tantric Symbol of Cosmic Unity*. London: Thames and Hudson, 1979.

Zimmer, Heinrich. *Artistic Form and Yoga in the Sacred Images of India*. Princeton: Princeton University Press, 1984.

Vastu Yantra Guidebook: Using Vedic Sacred Geometry to Balance Spatial Energies. Free pdf book available at www.transcendencedesign.com.

audio recordings

Jacob, Suzanne, Jürgen Wloka, Hans Kaufmann, Henry T. Dom. *Vastu-Purusha, Harmony of Space*. 2004. Compact disc.

Pruess, Craig and Ananda. *Sacred Chants of Shiva*. 2002. Compact disc.

Pruess, Craig, Bhanmati Narsimhan, Urmila Devi Goenka. *Sacred Chants of Devi*. 1998. Compact disc.

Thompson, Dr. Jeffrey. *Sri Yantra*. 1994. Compact disc.

CDs available through www.transcendencedesign.com

recommended stress management and meditation courses

Sri Sri Ravi Shankar

The Art of Living Foundation

800.897.5913

www.artofliving.org

Sudarshan Kriya, The Art of Living Course, and Sahaj Samadhi Meditation

vastu courses

American University of Mayonic Science & Technology

www.aumscience.com

aumcourses@aumscience.com

Dr. V. Ganapati Sthapati

Vaastu Vedic Research Foundation

Chennai, India

www.vastuved.com

jyotish

American College of Vedic Astrology (ACVA)

800.900.6595

www.vedicastrology.org

ayurveda

www.artofliving.ca/ayurvedicretreat.asp

http://artdevivre.artofliving.org

Wonderful Ayurveda clinic at the Quebec Art of Living Ashram

Ayurveda Organics and Om Organics

888.550.VEDA

www.omorganics.com

Ayurvedic supplements and *tulsi* teas

Banyan Botanicals

888.829.5722

www.banyanbotanicals.com

Mostly organic, non-irradiated herbs

Maharishi Ayurveda

www.mapi.com

Ayurvedic supplements and information

Vaidya R. K. Mishra

www.vaidyamishra.com

Ayurvedic Transdermal Marma System

Ayurvedic consultations, courses, and products

Glossary

AGNI: fire; one of the five elements, predominant in the southeast; also the name of a Vedic deity.

AKASHA: space; the most subtle of the five elements, predominant in the center of a building.

AYADI GANANAM: mathematical calculations used in Vastu to fit the vibration of the individual to the building, jewelry, or other constructed designs.

AYURVEDA: the science of life; health system from the Vedic tradition in India.

BHUMI: earth; one of the five elements, predominant in the southwest.

BINDU: the junction point that represents the entire universe and through which the seen world is manifested from the unmanifest Source.

BRAHMASTHAN: the center of the building and each room, which should be kept clean and open.

CHAKRA: wheel, circle; subtle but powerful main energy or nerve centers in the body.

CH'I or **CHI**: life-energy; the Chinese term for prana, known mostly in the West because of interest in Oriental medicine and Feng Shui.

DEVA: god, deity, devata, impulse of creative intelligence with specialized energies and attributes.

DEVATA: impulse of creative intelligence with specialized energies and attributes; guardians of different *padas* of the *Vastu Purusha Mandala*.

DOSHA: one of the three basic types of bodily constitutions according to Ayurveda: *vata*, *pitta*, and *kapha*.

FENG SHUI: China's system of design and placement; literally means "wind and water."

GANESHA: elephant-headed god associated with Vastu measurements, who is the remover of obstacles and protector of women; son of Devi (Mother Divine). Ganesha is invoked at the beginning of new ventures.

GARBHA-GRIHA: innermost chamber of a temple, womb-chamber.

GRAHA: planet or celestial luminary; there are nine in Vedic astrology (Jyotish).

HINDI: a major contemporary language of India.

HINDU: common term referring to *Sanatana Dharma*, the collection of religious ideals, guidelines, deities, and systems of worship that developed in India.

JALA: water; one of the five elements, predominant in the northeast.

JYOTISH: the lunar system of astrology from India's Vedic tradition. Mayan, the founder of Vastu, wrote one of the first Jyotish texts.

KALASH or **KALASHA**: pot; finial. Rooftop kalashes are sacred symbols and energy tools that bless and channel sacred energy into the home.

KAPHA: one of the three *doshas* in Ayurveda.

KOLAM: ritual rice powder drawings done by the women of a household on the threshold of the home at dawn to bless and protect the home.

LAKSHMI: goddess of good luck, good fortune, prosperity, and abundance. There are eight aspects of Lakshmi.

Eightfold Lakshmi

MANDALA: circle; cosmic diagram; a type of sacred geometry from the Vedic tradition that is also found in Buddhism, especially Tibetan Buddhism.

MANGAL: Sanskrit name for the planet Mars, planetary lord of the south.

MANTRA: sound vibration used to create a specific effect that allows the mind to transcend or to honor a deity or planet in order to achieve greater support in life.

MARMA: hidden; secret. There are *marmas* on the human body and on the body of Purusha on the *Vastu Purusha Mandala*.

MOTHER WALL: the basic square or rectangular plan of a building designed according to Vastu.

NAVAGRAHAS: nine planets or celestial bodies of the Vedic system of astrology, Jyotish: Jupiter, Ketu, sun, Venus, Mars, Rahu, Saturn, moon, and Mercury.

PADA: foot (as body part); section of the grid pattern of the *Vastu Purusha Mandala*.

PANCHABHUTAS: the five elements: earth, water, fire, air, and space.

PITTA: one of the three *doshas* in Ayurveda.

PRAKRITI: nature perceived as a feminine principle.

PRANA: life force or subtle life energy that flows in nature; obtained from food, water, breath, etc.

PRANAPRATISHTHA: an activation ceremony that breathes life into and/or acknowledges the divine energies residing in a *yantra* or image.

PRANAYAMA: breathing techniques that energize and purify; frequently translated as "breath control." Sri Sri Ravi Shankar translates *pranayama* as "housed in the dimension of the breath."

PRASAD: a blessed gift from the divine, usually some sort of sweet or other item given out after it has been offered in a *puja* or *yagya*. *Prasad* is also distributed by spiritual teachers or *gurus*.

PUJA: ceremony honoring the divine; a sacred performance involving words, gestures, offerings, and intentions.

PURUSHA: Cosmic Being; the Universal Self, the transcendental principle of masculine divine.

RASA: "essence," "juice"; emotional flavors that are evoked by the arts.

SADHANA: spiritual practices such as meditation, yoga, and *pranayama*.

SANSKRIT: ancient language from India considered by many to be the blueprint of creation.

SHAKTI: a name of the Goddess; dynamic power of the Universal Mother, the Feminine Divine; tangible spiritual energy.

SHANI: Sanskrit name for the planet Saturn, planetary lord of the west.

SHASTRA: text; sacred science; technical treatise.

SHILPA: sculpture; sculpture created according to Vastu guidelines.

SHILPI: temple sculptor; a sculptor trained in traditional Vastu sculptural art.

SHIVA: masculine divine characterized by purity, innocence, and transcendence; also known as the creator and destroyer or transformer of the universe, although Brahma is more specifically the creator.

SOMA: a specific healing, nourishing substance; a category of medicinal plants; finest, most subtle product of the nervous system and digestive system; a cooling substance associated with the moon; a *pada devata* on the *Vastu Purusha Mandala*.

Shiva

SRI: Mother Divine, the Goddess, Lakshmi; bliss.

STHAPATYA VEDA: that part of the Vedas referring to architecture and design; Vastu.

SUNDARI: beauty; the goddess Tripura Sundari, beauty of the three worlds.

SURYA: the sun in Vedic astrology, planetary lord of the east.

TAMIL: language spoken in the Indian state of Tamil Nadu; the ancient language in which many Vastu texts were written.

TANTRA: an approach to enlightenment, growth of consciousness, and union with the divine that embraces the physical and honors the Feminine.

TULSI: holy basil; an herb sacred to Krishna.

UPANISHAD: a particular group of Vedic texts; literally "sitting nearby."

VAASTU: humanly built forms that are filled with space energy.

VAMSA DANDA: spine or thread of light; a vital feature of a Vastu house that energizes it by allowing *prana*, light, and energy to move into a building from the front door and connect with the outside again through a back door or window that is directly across from the entrance.

VASTU: energy, "the space that fills that form or dwelling," "substance that . . . exists eternally" (Sthapati). Although *Vaastu* is technically the correct term for buildings that embody space, *Vastu* is the usually seen name for India's spiritually and scientifically based system of architecture, design, and sacred space.

VATA: one of the three *doshas* in Ayurveda.

VAYU: wind, air; one of the five elements.

VEDA: sacred imperishable knowledge.

VEDIC ASTROLOGY: Jyotish, the lunar system of astrology from the Vedic tradition in India.

VIDYA: knowledge; science.

VISHNU: that aspect of the masculine divine trinity that is in charge of maintenance of the universe.

VISHWAKARMAN: the celestial architect; sometimes associated or equated with Mayan.

YANTRA: sacred diagram that contains the energy of a deity; an abstraction or archetypal image in mandala form that connects the viewer or worshipper with cosmic energies; sacred geometry from the Vedic tradition in India.

YOGA: union; physical postures; a name for the entire system of achieving union with the divine, including meditation.

YONI: the eight directional lines of energy that radiate out from the center of the *Brahmasthan*; a sacred term for the female genitals.

Notes

section one

1. Bachelard, *The Poetics of Space,* 53–54. Trans. Maria Jolas.
2. Finlay, *Color: A Natural History of the Palette,* 271.

section two

1. Sthapati, *Architecture of Sthapatya Veda,* 266.
2. Ibid., 289–290.
3. Kramrisch, *The Hindu Temple,* 6.
4. Ibid., 7.
5. Sthapati, *Building Architecture of Sthapatya Veda,* 124.
6. Swintzell, "Bupingeh: The Pueblo Plaza," *El Palacio* 94.2 (winter 1988):15.
7. Sthapati, *Architecture of Sthapatya Veda,* 9.
8. Coomaraswamy, *Christian and Oriental Philosophy of Art,* 18.
9. Mookerjee and Khanna, *The Tantric Way,* 41.
10. Frawley, *Tantric Yoga and the Wisdom Goddesses*, 91.
11. Poem by the author, first published in *Seeds of Unfolding*, Volume IV, Number 2, Spring 1987.
12. Poem by the author, first published in *The Art of Living Journal*, Winter 1994: 8.
13. Frawley, *Ayurvedic Healing*, 314, 252, 241.
14. Sthapati, *Building Architecture of Sthapatya Veda*, 203.
15. Bachelard, *The Poetics of Space,* 35.

section three

1. Kramrisch, *The Hindu Temple,* 22, 42.
2. Huyler, *Painted Prayers: Women's Art in Village India*, 161.
3. Nagarajan, "Hosting the Divine: The Kolam in Tamilnadu," *Mud, Mirror and Thread,* 203.

section four

1. Bachelard, *the Poetics of Space,* 79.
2. Dagens, ed., *Mayamata*, 79.
3. Swami Muktananda, qtd. in Rubinov-Jacobson, *Drinking Lightning: Art, Creativity, and Transformation,* 71.
4. Khanna, *Yantra: The Tantric Symbol of Cosmic Unity*, 98.
5. Ibid., 99.
6. Hymn from *Rig Veda* translated by the author and David Frawley.

Bibliography

Acharya, Prasanna Kumar. *Indian Architecture According to Mānasārā-Śilpaśāstra*. Vol. II. New Delhi: Oriental Books Reprint Corp., 1981.

Bachelard, Gaston. *The Poetics of Space*. Boston: Beacon Press, 1964.

Campbell, Joseph with Bill Moyers. *The Power of Myth*. New York: Doubleday, 1988.

Coomaraswamy, Ananda K. *Christian and Oriental Philosophy of Art*. New York: Dover, 1956.

Cooper, J.C. *An Illustrated Encyclopaedia of Traditional Symbols*. London: Thames and Hudson, 1978.

Dagens, Bruno, ed. and trans. *Mayamata: Treatise of Housing, Architecture and Iconography*. Vol. I and II. New Delhi: Indira Gandhi National Centre for the Arts/Delhi: Motilal Banarsidass Publishers, 1994.

Feuerstein, Georg, Subhash Kak and David Frawley. *In Search of the Cradle of Civilization: New Light on Ancient India*. Wheaton, IL: Quest Books, 1995.

Finlay, Victoria. *Color: A Natural History of the Palette*. New York: Ballantine, 2003.

Fisher, Nora. *Mud, Mirror and Thread: Folk Traditions of Rural India*. Middletown, NJ: Grantha/Museum of International Folk Art/Ahmedabad, India: Grantha, 1993.

Frawley, David. *Ayurvedic Healing: A Comprehensive Guide*. Salt Lake City: Passage Press, 1989.

———. *Gods, Sages and Kings: Vedic Secrets of Ancient Civilization*. Salt Lake City: Passage Press, 1991.

———. *Tantric Yoga and the Wisdom Goddesses: Spiritual Secrets of Ayurveda*. Twin Lakes, WI: Lotus Press, 1994.

Goswamy, B. N. *Essence of Indian Art*. San Francisco: Asian Art Museum of San Francisco, 1986.

Huyler, Stephen P. *Painted Prayers: Women's Art in Village India*. New York: Rizzoli, 1994.

Kandinsky, Wassily. *Concerning the Spiritual in Art*. (1912) trans. M.T.H. Sadler. New York: Dover, 1977.

Khanna, Madhu. *Yantra: The Tantric Symbol of Cosmic Unity*. London: Thames and Hudson, 1979.

Kramrisch, Stella. *The Hindu Temple*. 1946. Columbia, MO: South Asia Books, 1991.

Lad, Vasant and David Frawley. *The Yoga of Herbs: An Ayurvedic Guide to Herbal Medicine*. Santa Fe: Lotus Press, 1986.

Mitter, Partha. *Indian Art*. Oxford: Oxford UP, 2001.

Mookerjee, Ajit. *Kali: The Feminine Force*. New York: Destiny Books, 1988.

———. *Tantra Art: Its Philosophy and Physics*. Basel, Switzerland: Ravi Kumar, 1971.

———. *Tantra Asana: A Way to Self-Realization*. New York: Wittenborn/Basel, Switzerland: Ravi Kumar, 1971.

———. *Yoga Art*. Boston: New York Graphic Society, 1975.

——— and Madhu Khanna. *The Tantric Way*. Boston: New York Graphic Society, 1977.

Rubinov-Jacobson, Philip. *Drinking Lightning: Art, Creativity, and Transformation*. Boston: Shambhala, 2000.

Schmieke, Marcus. *Vastu: The Origin of Feng Shui*. Great Britain: Goloka Books Ltd., 2002.

Shearer, Alistair. *The Hindu Vision: Forms of the Formless*. London: Thames & Hudson, 1993.

Sthapati, Ganapati. *Building Architecture of Sthapatya Veda*. Chennai, India: Dakshinaa Publishing House, 2001.

———. *Temples of Space-Science*. Madras: Vastu Vedic Research Foundation, 1996.

———. *Vastu Purusha Mandala: Energy Grid for Building Layouts*. Chennai, India: Dakshinaa Publishing House, 2000.

Swintzell, Rina. "Bupingeh: The Pueblo Plaza." *El Palacio* 94.2 (Winter 1988): 14–19.

Walker, Alice. *Living by the Word*. New York: Harvest Books/Harcourt Brace, 1989.

Witherspoon, Bill. *Art and Technology*. Unpublished essay.

Zimmer, Heinrich. *Artistic Form and Yoga in the Sacred Images of India*. Princeton: Princeton University Press, 1984.

Photography Credits

Index